COMPARATIVE URBAN RESEARCH

PERSPECTIVES IN URBAN GEOGRAPHY
Volume Two

Concept's International Series in Geography

No. 1 Perspectives in Agricultural Geography (In Five Volumes) Edited by Noor Mohammad

No. 2 Perspectives in Geomorphology (In Four Volumes) Edited by S.H. Sharma

No. 3 Perspectives in Urban Geography Edited by C.S. Yadav

1. New Directions in Urban Geography
2. Comparative Urban Research
3. Comparative Urbanization: City Growth and Change

4A. Models in Urban Geography (Theoretical)

4B. Models in Urban Geography (Mathematical)

5. Urban Research Methods: Central Place, Hierarchical and City Size Models
6. Contemporary City Ecology
7. Slums, Urban Decline and Revitalization
8. Contemporary Urban (Issues)
9. Rural-Urban Fringe
10. Morphology of Towns
11. Cities and Housing
12. Perceptual and Cognative Image of the City
13. Urban Economics
14. City Planning: Problems and Prospects
15. City Planning: Administration and Participation

16A. Urban Planning and Policies: Reorientation of Policy Norms

16B. Urban Planning and Policies: Cross-Cultural Urban Policies

Concept's International Series in Geography No. 3

Perspectives in Urban Geography

Volume Two

COMPARATIVE URBAN RESEARCH

Edited by

C.S. YADAV

CONCEPT PUBLISHING COMPANY, NEW DELHI-110 059

First Published 1986
Reprinted 2007

Published and Printed by
Ashok Kumar Mittal
Concept Publishing Company
A/15-16, Commercial Block, Mohan Garden
New Delhi-110059 (INDIA)
Phones : 25351460, 25351794 *Fax* : 091-11-25357103
Email : publishing@conceptpub.com

PREFACE

NATURE OF URBAN GEOGRAPHY

THERE are several studies on urban geography which reveal that, as a major sub-discipline, it has a long tail but a short body. However, the spectrum is so vast and broad that researchers are able to make general statements in defence of its conception, philosophy, nature and orientation. Urban geography today encompasses and interfaces with various disciplines which are interested in urban studies. As an introduction to this series, our task here is to make an attempt to briefly review the development of geographical interest in various aspects of cities.

There are several reviews of the early development of urban geography which have been dealt with by Berry and Harton (1970)[1] and Carter (1974).[2] Berry and Harton in their book, *Geographical Perspective on Urban System*, have made an attempt to introduce readers to its present-day status. They have clearly resolved that "the formative years of the social science in the late nineteenth century and early twentieth century were also the years in which urban studies first developed,"[3] thus providing the context for the geography's emerging interest in cities. However, the emergence of urban studies dates back to the writing of Greek scholars, but as a sub-discipline, it has reached its present-day status only in the past 30 years.

In their historical perspective the works on urban geography show that the pre-20th century studies primarily concerned themselves with themes of location, size and shape of the cities. The initial findings were strongly subjective, descriptive and dependent more on observation such as the works of Hassert (1907)[4] and Blanchard (1911).[5] In the succeeding years the conceptual framework of site and situation was criticized by Aurousseau (1924)[6] and Crowe (1938)[7], their conception being that cities were not inanimate objects in landscape, but also organic elements which involved people and their movements. The morphologist, later in 1960, truly brought the indigenous line of evolution in the sphere of urban geography and studies on the build-up fabric of cities (Conzone, 1960).[8] Smails (1955)[9] constituted the prime base of urban geography, which remained articulated without any major conceptual change till early 1960s. The studies on the morphological aspects of the urban system were influenced by external forces, consequently the methodological frameworks got impetus within the discipline. At this juncture the evolution of concepts was not based on environment but took shelter under the umbrella of economics of location, and incorporated analysis of land values and rents, and the concept of nodality and accessibility. These concepts were derived from the economic theories of Cooley (1894)[10], Weber (1899),[11] and Hurd (1903).[12]

The Chicago School of Urban Ecology hastened the evolution of urban geography. In his monumental work Park (1925)[13] developed the idea of order and analysis of towns. Further, a powerful thrust and much of the rationale was provided to the studies of urban geography by the Central Place Theory of Christallar (1933).[14]

The impact of the satistical method was powerful and it brought rapid and enormous changes in the field of urban geography. It also brought new insights into the development and application of urban geography towards increased quantification. Brian J. Berry, a pioneer in the field, analysed the spatial order, size and location of towns and cities. There was widespread use of innovative techniques to explore the nature of urban problems, hypotheses were tested, new theories propounded and old theories remodelled. The statistical methods were put to a variety of uses. Smith (1965)[15] evaluated the classification of settlements; Berry and Garrison (1956)[16] examined the utility of the rank-size rule for urban populations. The models of Park and Burgess (1925),[17] Harris and Ullman (1945)[18] and Homar Hoyt (1939)[19] were tested and re-examined by various geographers.

A new impetus to urban geography came from social area analysis which was initially propounded by Shevky and Bell (1955)[20] and later on this provided a basis for factorial ecology. The collaboration of this stream in urban geography was offered by Berry (1971),[21] Herbert (1972)[22] and Johnston (1971).[23] As a consequence of these thrusts in geography after 1960, the techniques of investigation were sharpened and this has provided the basis for a scientific explanation of cities. Attempts were made to introduce new theories and frame laws to make the explanation of events more rational and logical. Sophisticated models were propounded as urban geography entered a new era of rationalizing the subject matter of urban studies on the basis of new philosophies, new concepts, new theories, new methodologies and applications.

However, the status of contemporary urban geography has been elevated only recently by the behavioural approach. The studies of perception and cognition which have a long tradition in physiology were first introduced into the field of geography by Lynch (1960),[24] Dowson and Stea (1973)[25] Gould and White (1974).[26] At present there is a sudden spurt in the studies on the subject with a new paradigm. But the full impact of behavioural approaches upon urban geography has yet to be realized.

The aim of this series is to seek reorientation of the discipline strengthened by new philosophies, methodologies, subject matters or application. The series has been arranged in such a way that all contemporary view points are covered comprehensively. Hopefully, this series will inspire researchers to appreciate the work already done by geographers in studying cities. Geography by nature seems to be a synthesizing field of inquiry. As such we have made an endeavour to combine some of the otherwise disparate facts garnered by other disciplines in such a manner that we can gain a better understanding of the urban system. The study of urban geography is essential if we are to analyse the human consequences of the settlements in which we live. It is useful to planners, decision makers in government and corporations and also to each one of us as citizens. Finally, it gives us a perspective on what may be happening to our cities and to the nature.

To achieve the above goal only those contributions with

originality and contrasting viewpoints were selected for inclusion in this series. In doing so the editor does not wish to compete with the journals in the field in which innovative research and methodological aspects are presented. But he does wish to convey, and convey with conviction, that significant researches are being undertaken in the different branches of urban geography and in other allied disciplines. The present series is an attempt to provide a selective reappraisal and rigorous examination of the assumptions and the urge to disseminate new knowledge created by the mutual interaction. Emphasis is also placed on the conceptualization and theorization of the subject matter so that general laws may emerge. A conscious effort has been to organize the series in such a way that it reflects the philosophical approach parallel to that of the behavioural school. Finally, a vigorous attempt has been made to demonstrate throughout the series now geographers are basically involved in solving the urban problems.

REFERENCES

1. Berry and Harton, *Geographic Perspectives on Urban Systems: With Integrated Readings*, New Jersey, Prentice Hell, INC, Englewood Cliffs, 1970
2. Carter, *The Study of Urban Geography*, Edward Arnold, London, 1974.
3. Berry and Harton, 1970.
4. Hassert, K., *Die Stadte Geographisch Betrachect*, Leipzig, 1907.
5. Blanchard, R., *Grenoble: Etude De Geographic Urbanine*, Paris, 1911.
6. Aurousseau, M., "Recent Contributions to Geography: A Review," *Geographical Review*, 1924, 14, p. 444.
7. Crowe., P.R., "On Progress in Geography," *Scottish Geographical* Magazfne, 1938, 54-1-19.
8. Conzone, M.R.G., "The Plan Analysis of an English City Centre," Ink. Norkorg (Ed), *Proceedings of I.G.U. Symposium on Urban Geography*, C.W.K. Gleerup, Lund, 1962.
9. Smails, A.E., "The Urban Mes of England and Wales," *Transactions and Papers*, Institute of British Geographers 1946, 11, 85, p. 101.
10. Cooley, C.H., "The Theory of Transportation," *Publications of the American Economic Association*, 1894, 9, p. 5-7
11. Weber, A.F., *The Growth of Cities in the Nineteenth Century: A Study in Statistics*, New York, 1899.

12. Hurd, R., *Principles of City Land Values: New York Record and Guide*, 1903, p. 19-21.
13. Park, R.E., "Suggestions for the Investigation of Human Behaviour in an Urban Environment," in R.E. Park, E.W. Burgess, R.D. Mackenizie (eds), *The City*, University of Chicago Press, 1925.
14. Christallar, W., *Central Place in Southern Germany*, Gustar Fischer, Teno, 1933.
15. Smith, R.M.T., "Method and Purpose in Functional Town Classification," *Annals of the Association of American Geographers*, 1965, 55, pp. 539-548.
16. Carrison, W.L., "Applicability of Statistical Inference to Geographical Research," *Geographical Review*, 1956, 46, 427, 429.
17. Burgess, E.W., "The Growth of City," in R.E. Park, E.W. Burgess and R.D. Mackenizie (eds), *The City*, University of Chicago Press, 1925.
18. Ullman, E.L., "The Nature of Cities," *Annals*, American Academy of Political and Social Science, 1945, 242, 7-17.
19. Hoyt, H., *The Structure and Growth of Residential Neighbourhoods in American Cities*, Washington, Federal Housing Administration 1939.
20. Shevky, E. and Bell, W., *Social Area Analysis*, Stamford University Press, Stamford, 1955.
21. Berry, B.J.L. (ed), "Comparative Factorial Ecology," *Economic Geographic (Supplement)*, 1971, 47.
22. Herbert, D.T., *Urban Geography: A Social Perspective*, David and Charles, Newton Abbot, 1972.
23. Johnston, *Urban Residential Pattern*, Bell, London, 1971.
24. Lynch, *Image of the City*, Massachusetts, Cambirdge, 1960.
25. Dowson and Stea, "Image and Environment", Chicago and London, 1973.
26. Gould and White, R., *Mental Maps*, London, 1974.

ACKNOWLEDGEMENT

We Thank Editors Gerd-Michael Hellstern, Frithjof Spreer Hellmut Wollmann *Heft 2 Vol. II* for their permission to use material from "Applied Urban Research" Proceedings of the European Meeting on Applied Urban Research, Essen Oct. 1981.

CONTENTS

PREFACE v

ACKNOWLEDGEMENT x

LIST OF CONTRIBUTORS xv

1. Introduction 1
—*C.S. Yadav*

SECTION ONE
LEARNING FROM COMPARATIVE URBAN RESEARCH

2. Some Methodological and Technological Issues in Comparative Urban Analysis
—*Karl-Heinz Simon* and *Bernd Hamm* 23

3. Cross-Cultural Studies on Urban Structure: Research Goals, Historical Development, Results, Current Problems
—*Burkhard Hofmeister* 37

4. Progress in Comparative Urban Research
—*Jurgen Friedrichs* 53

5. On the Limits of Social Ecological Explanations in Comparative Research
—*Erling Berge* 59

6. Policy Analysis as a Starting Point for Comparative Studies
—*Alan Norton* 67

7. Structural Change in Old Industrial Agglomerations: First Experiences from a Comparative Research Project
—*Klaus R. Kunzmann* 85

8. Some Remarks to the Methodological Problems of International Comparative Studies on Residents' Resistance in Urban Renewal
—*Harald Bodenschatz, Volker Heise* and *Jochen Korfmacher* 107

9. Comment of Topic of the Internationalization of Urban Problems: Comparing Convergent International Trends
—*David C. Throns* 113

10. New Urban Policies for New Urban Realities
—*John D. Kasarda* 119

SECTION TWO

COMPARISON OF NATIONAL AND INTERNATIONL URBAN RESEARCH

11. Current Research Trends in the European Countries: Premises for Transnational and Comparative Urban and Regional Research
—*Jacques Robert* 137

12. Evaluating Urban and Regional Research in the Federal Republic of Germany
—*Horst M. Bolting* 149

13. Trends in Applied Urban Research in Germany
—*Hellmut Wollmann* 157

14. Urban Research in France
—*Jacques Pernelle* 167

15. Urban Community Research in Switzerland: Past and Future
—*Erwin Zimmermann* 173

16. Urban Research in the Netherlands
—Henk Voogd 181

17. Urban Social Research in Yugoslavia
—Zdravko Mlinar 185

18. Applied Urban Research in Austria
—Wolf Huber 191

19. Metropolitan Planning and Problems in Europe: The Contribution of the Vienna Centre
—Armando Montanari 197

20 The Basis of Urban Research in Japan
—Hachiro Nakamura 209

INDEX 215

LIST OF CONTRIBUTORS

Erling Berge: Institute of Applied Social Research, OSLO 2, Norway.

Harald Bodenschatz: Technical University, Berlin.

Horst M. Bolting: Federal Ministry of Regional Planning and Urban Development, 5300 Bonn 2, Federal Republic of Germany.

Jurgen Friedrichs: University of Hamburg.

Bernd Hamm: Department of Social Science, University of Trier, Germany.

Volker Heise: Technical University, Berlin.

Burkhard Hofmeister: Institut fuer Geographie Technische Universitaet, Berlin Budapester Strasse 44/46, D. 1000, Berlin, 30.

Wolf Huber: Kommunalwissenschaftliches Dokumentation-szentrum (KDZ) Vienna (Austria).

John D. Kasarda: University of North Carolina at Chapel Hill, U.S.A.

Jochen Korfmacher: Technical University, Berlin.

Klaus R. Kunzmann: Institut fur Raumplanung, Universitat Dortmund, Brian McLoughlin Manchester Liverpool.

Zdravko Mlinar: Faculty for Sociology, Political Science and Journalism, Ljubljana, Yugoslavia.

Armando Montanari: Scientific Secretary at the Vienna Centre and Co-ordinator of the project "The Costs of Urban Growth (CURB)" and "the Project Turin International Grunangergasse 2, P.O. Box 974, A 1011 Veinna, Austria.

Hachiro Nakamura: Tsukuba University, Japan.

Alan Nortan: Institute of Local Government Studies, University of Birmingham, Birmingham.

Jacques Pernelle: Direction de l' Urbanisme et des Paysages Ministere de l' Urbanisme et du Logement, France.

Jacques Robert: European Research Network, Post Box 96950, The Hague, The Netherland.

Karl-Heinz Simon: Department of Social Science, University of Trier, Germany.

David C. Throns
Department of Sociology, University of Canterbury, Christchurch, New Zealand.

Henk Voogd: Technische Hogeschool Te Delft, University of Technology, 134, Julinalaan, P.O.Box. 5 Delft, The Netherland.

Hellmut Wollmann: Centre for Social Research, Free University, Berlin.

C.S. Yadav: Department of Geography, Bhagat Singh College, Delhi University, New Delhi.

Erwin Zimmermann: Swiss Federal Institute of Technology, Lausanne, Switzerland.

ONE

C.S. YADAV

INTRODUCTION

WE CAN start with an assumption that the attraction of the city as a subject for analysis to the student of urban geography is readily understandable. It is a truism that increasing millions in every part of the world are dependent for the quality of their lives, for their survival on cities. Therefore, city is a purveyor of essential services, it is a source of basic amenities and of opportunities for personal development and seems to be an instrument for maintenance of law and order. As such it is imperative for urban geographers to deepen their understanding about cities and their problems, about the process of urbanization and how to control spontaneous settlements. To achieve these ends we have to exploit fully the contribution of comparative urban research. The two decades since World War II have witnessed a remarkable growth in the use of comparative analytical techniques to explore the complex character of the cities (Daland, 1969).[1] It is believed that till early 1960s, the available material on comparative urban analysis was limited, scattered and, in many cases, fugitive (Walton, 1976).[2] Since then it has been observed that the field of comparative urban analysis is growing fast and there is enough evidence to justify that the field is developing on a variety of fronts, as is clearly evident from the books such as *The Human consequences of Urbanization* (Berry, 1973),[3] *Modernization, Urbanization and Urban Crisis* (Germani, 1973),[4] *Urbanism, Urbanization and Change: Comparative Perspective* (Medows, 1969)[5] *Urbanism in World Perspective*

(Fara, 1969),[6] *The City in Newly Developing Countries* (Brease, 1969),[7] *Comparative Community Politics* (Clark, 1974),[8] *An Urban World* (Tilly, 1974)[9] and *Comparative Urban Structure Studies in the Ecology of Cities* (Schwirian, 1974),[10] *Comparative Urban Research* (Daland, 1969).[11] *The City in Comparatative perspective* (Walton, 1969),[12] and appearance of Journal issues devoted primarily to comparative urban research, e.g. *Economic Geography*.[13] *The New Atlantic*,[14] *Urban Affairs Quarterly* (Nov. 1972[15] and Feb. 1973), and an increasing number of articles in both disciplinary journals and special focus journals. A review of this literature reveals that comparative urban research provides for scholars a lively forum for their activities, projects and research.

PROBLEMS

The comparative analysis has contributed in an important way to the enlarging of our understanding of the dynamics of modernization throughout the world. It has provided better clues to the students of older, industrialized societies seeking to explore the changing patterns of behaviour (Daland, 1969).[16] Yet the application of comparative urban studies has tended to lag behind its use in studying the complex problems of growing metropolis. We have failed to exploit fully the contribution of comparative urban research and afford to continue tolerating that failure. However, 'The paucity of comparative urban research is not due to an indifference on the part of the social scientist, but to the absence of (flow of) comparable or standardized information from one country to another, and to technical problems, presented by this deficiency. The units of observation themselves, that is, "Cities" and "Towns," have not been standardized, nor have we information on a representative sample of those for the world as a whole. Most of our data pertained to the "Cities" of the West, although just as many "Cities" are found in the rest of the world. Furthermore, the structure of urban communities has changed with increasing urbanization, a change that has gone further in some countries than in others. This dynamic element has meant that definitions of urban places adequate for one region or time have not been suitable for another region or time.'[17]

There has, on the one hand, been excessive fragmentation of comparative urban research and on the other, there is little agreement on what is "Comparative", the term being applied to everything from research done in some foreign or non-native setting to carefully controlled field experiments or stratified case comparisons (Walton, 1976).[18] Thus the great majority of comparative urban research has been parochial. The parochialism of urban research is reflected when researchers venture into "foreign" settings with a prefabricated set of theoretical and methodological tools which presuppose the order and meaning of the events, e.g. social area analaysis and urban ecology are the venerable traditions in U.S. urban studies. Theoretically this approach relies unequally on dominance and competition. The main assumptions of this approach are that patterns of land area and urban social structure are the outcome of competitive forces in the marketplace. The distribution of different groups and classes in urban space is a function of their unequal resources and value choices. Now these assumptions are challenged in the USA and they seem to be much less credible when applied to Third World cities whose social structure pertains to colonial dominance.

The solution to this parochialism lies in more extensive work, on a longer scale with a broader range of theoretical viewpoints. The myopia of parochialism can be constrained by a critical examination of comparative works with a presumption that our present knowledge about it is inadequate to explain urban forms and processes, because it has either precluded examination of fundamental casual forces by focussing on special cases or because it has misinterpreted those casual forces.

SOLUTION

It is quite obvious that we need to examine some alternative viewpoint to explore and suggest in favour of a comparative urban analysis. Researchers have formed an impression that proliferation of comparative urban research is an unmixed blessing.

To resolve the antagonistic viewpoints this should be promptly qualified. This activity has led to an excessive exfragmentation of comparative work. Researchers from various streams with separate interests and with little coordination have variously construed comparative urbanism as the study of migration, and migrant adaptation, social ecology, land use planning, economic function, location theory and citizen's participation, lifestyles and modernization and the like. The essence of this observation affirms that there is no field of comparative urban analysis as distinct from disparateness of disciplines. J. Walton and L.H. Wasocti (1976)[19] correctly concluded that this is unavoidably necessary or even desirable because to explore the complex nature of cities we need an urban anthropology to study settlement patterns, an urban geography to study location, an urban political science to study government and citizens's participation, an urban sociology, an urban economist, an urban psychologist and so on. This disciplinary Balkanization implies a fundamental fragmentation of information and there is nothing distinctively urban to be understood or explained, rather the urban milieu is merely a setting for the study of a variety of processes defined by other criterion. Assuming that some principled base could be established for urban phenomenon with greater regularity or in more intensified ways. It should then be possible to expand the field significantly by integrating various approaches with a common framework or a limited set of competing frameworks particularly towards coherent and systematic agreed upon goals.

THE LOGIC OF COMPARISONS

When a researcher makes a choice to analyse the comparability of urban communities he obviously assumes three alternatives. The first and most qualified assumption reveals that there are certain universals to be applied to urbanization and urbanism. It is a well-recognized fact that cities are characterized by relatively greater size, density and heterogeneity of the population. This situation leads to segmentation of urban communities. The conditions are repetitive from one place to another which results in a spurt of studies on urbanization in similar cultural regions.

Contrary to this assumption the second assumption qualifies that there are no universals which hold true of urban communities and that, therefore, there is no basis on which to compare them as a class. This position is more commonly implicit rather than explicit (Daland).[20] However, writers assert, for example, that comparisons are valid within Western Europe or within the Third World, but that comparisons between these areas can produce nothing useful because each area exhibits an entirely different cultural set-up, thus it is commonly believed that there is no basis for comparing large with small cities, cities in a federal system with cities in a unitary system or industrial with trading cities.

The third assumption with better acceptability has more application; it asserts that there is neither presence nor absence of universals. The answer becomes difficult in practice. However, it is clear as a methodological concept. The researcher is able to achieve comparison by controlling the variables through a careful selection of cities which are similar with respect to a number of variables. The comparability may be sought through selection of similar city types in a variety of cultural or structural settings. It may also be attained through observing the incidence of a given type or a series of events in a variety of cultural or structural settings. If great variability occurs within a culture, the comparability may be sought between nations of similar historical backgrounds, and when we observe uniformity within cultures comparability may be approched among nations of somewhat dissimilar backgrounds.

These observations, general questions as to what to compare, and there are many serious, thorny questions of how to compare cross nationally, cross culturally. How can we ascertain that we have compared the same thing given in our particular research objectives pose a serious problem to a researcher. The logic of comparisons to the rationale employed to support the claim that City A and City B have similarities or common properties or dissimilar along specified dimensions to allow meaningful, convergent, comparisons. As a convention the former is termed as a "Conceptual equivalence" (Sears, 1969)[21] and is considered a matter of inference, not of direct observation. When researchers attempt to study cross cultural variability in social reality, the problem is to design a research strategy or arrange existing data in such a fashion that it yield the most meaningful, appropriate generalization. This can be achieved only by means of comparative analysis which implies appropriate selection of units and levels of analysis and formulation of appropriate measures of conceptual equivalence across the regions being campared (Przeworski, 1970).[22]

It is a truism that most comparative studies begin with known differences among social systems and evaluate the effect of these differences on some other social phenomena which occur within these systems. Przeworski and Teune (1970)[23] have clearly analysed an alternative strategy for the comparativist. They suggest to take into account system differences as they are explained by observed social phenomena in the system. They postulate two research design strategies—most similar systems and most dissimilar systems. In the former which Naroll (1968)[24] has termed concomitant variation" systems which provides a base for optimal samples for comparisons.

FUTURE TASK

The comparative urban research contrary to earlier belief is a distinctive field of study. If this is so, one expects the contents of the field to be distinctive as well including its concepts, issues, data, method of analysis and findings. The importance of comparative urban research as compared with the study of national and international system of cross national and cross cultural analysis are both strategic and substantive. It has been noted that comparative urban studies are of intrinsic interest in the field of urban geography. Janet Abu Lughod[25] clearly stated that "comparative urban studies back up a bit from the ambitious task it has taken upon itself and sets more precise limits to its activities, limits which will distinguish legitimate comparisons from illegitimate comparisons given the present state of art." According to him comparative urban analysis is a complicated task, requiring knowledge of many more disciplines and facts than specialists are usually trained. Thus, it seems, it is a field of studies in its infancy and an enormous task remains to be done. However, contribution of such task to a deeper, logical understanding or urban process cannot be overestimated.

ABOUT THIS VOLUME

The primary objective of conducting a comparative urban analysis is to demonstrate the socio-spatial differentiation of a definite number of urban areas. Here the main objective of urban geographers is to seek cross sectional or cross longitudiual comparisons. The most valid assumption that explains the nature of comparative urban analysis is that urban areas are not ideosyncratic entities that are, at least to some extent, comparable in structure and development. If this is so, then urban geographers can contribute effectively towards concepts and strategies of comparative analysis.

In this volume those articles are included which demonstrate some order to the confused state of comparative analysis by organizing these essays around a set of developing properties. Each part of this volume provides some strong indications of where the field is moving, some sense of theoretical foundation that will lend coherence to a variety of urban problems. Most articles indicate new thinking about the nature of comparative research and trade its theoretical implications. This volume, however, is a modest attempt at providing a theoreticul basis for comparative urban studies and characterizes the kind of research that would follow from such a formulation.

The papers presented in this volume may be divided into two groups. The first group of papers deal with important scientific aspects and questions of comparative urban and regional research. They illustrate the theoretical framework concepts, strategies and methods involved and are of paramount importance for the future development of comparative urban research.

The second group of papers are those which document national and international research programmes on urban development. They particularly provide a useful survey of the goals and content of these programmes and describe the experience gained and the problems encountered in implementing them.

PART I: LEARNING FROM COMPARATIVE URBAN RESEARCH

Comparative urban research is a young discipline. Traditional goals, theories and methods have not yet been developed. The spectrum of research concepts and logic is, therefore, very broad. Kerl-Heinz Simon and Berni Hamm in their article, "Some Methodological and Technical Issues in Comparative Urban Analysis", have shown by their investigation that comparative urban research is descriptive and exploratory. They demonstrate that social ecology provides a fairly elaborated theoretical frame to understand urban development. In their article the authors have made an attempt to investigate the ecological structure of urban areas and have discussed selected methodological and technical problems in comparative analysis. They, have investigated the scope and methods of comparative urban analysis. The purpose of this analysis is to demonstrate and examine the differences and similarities in the social-spatial structure of the urban areas, the direction and intensity of change in the socio-spatial structure and the conditions of change. The authors suggest study of the classification of comparative urban analysis. They also emphasize levels of analysis and units of observation. They have showed the urgency to explore the dimensions of urban differentiations and selection of indicatiors. They also suggest use of a great variety of statistical methods and techniques for urban analysis which have been developed by social ecologists, regional scientists, qualitative geographers and by other disciplines.

Somewhere between the idiographic view of the individual city and the positive search for general rules applicable to the development and structure of all cities throughout the world, there is a medium scale of looking at groups of cities, e.g. those cities located in a distinct culture region. In each of the cultural regions the process of urbanization which is more or less the same throughout the world encounters different traditions and different societal, political, religious, economic and technological circumstances thus creating somewhat different urban structures. Burkhard Hofmeister in his article, "Cross Cultural Studies on Urban Structure: Research goals, Historical Development, Results, Current Problems", has made a vigorous attempt to demonstrate that research is conducted on various scales, e.g. the individual scale, the global scale and the corss cultural scale. However, in his paper the author has emphasized more the medium scale in which the goal is a group of cities in particular region similar to each other. According to the author, the inherent feature of any particular region, ideas and thought of their citizens and aspirations of people create them to work together to create their own settlement. The author clearly evaluates the development of the cultural-genetic approach in different cultural regions. He also gets an insight into the spatial frame of reference for the cultural-genetic approach. One of the outstanding features of the paper is that the author was unable to cite example studies of models of cultural genetic types of cities. He also evaluates the controversies in cross cultural studies of urban structure. Finally, the author himself concludes that cross cultural studies have been somewhat neglected for a long time and should be promoted in the future since they are of the greatest concern to urban geography in particular and to urban research in general.

Conducting comparative research implies a comparability of structures and processes. Thus the working hypothesis should identify regularities instead of assuming uniqueness of the element under study. Jurgen Friderichs in his paper "Process in Comparative Research", demonstrates that the most important condition for comparative urban research is to secure the comparability of the objects to be compared. The author doubts if we can view cities and countries as unique in history and structure comparison in its strickest sense. He believes it is not possible. He cautions the researcher that if he wishes to compare he has to work with hypotheses to find regularities, hypothesize, assuming comparability. This hypotheses require to take into account variables, which may be found in one country or one city only. The author presumes that comparative research may be directed;

1. To find regularities in the structure and development;
2. Isolating the effects of the specific economy, social and political conditions;
3. Change in the sub-areas of a city;

4. Types of certain planning solution in different policy fields like urban renewal, ethnic participation.

According to the author not only trends, reactions may be studied. He directs that temporal, spatial and social classifications will help to classify the comparison. He highlights some of the most urgent problems to improve future comparative research. These are:

1. Historical vs Deductive-nomological Laws.
2. Urban Succession Models.
3. Generality of Theories.
4. Specification of Constructs and indicators.
5. Level of Analysis.
6. Use of Special Research Approaches for Comparative Research.

While conducting the comparative urban research, some important steps and a tentative solution may be suggested.

In comparative research as elsewhere the important word is research. The comparative part just indicates one way of doing research. Erling Berge in his article, "On the Limits of Social Ecological Explanations in Comparative Research", clearly reveals that a socio-ecological explanation in comparative research is concerned with the variations in the inter-relations among the variables of the ecological complex.

The author propounds that inadequacies of the theory have created the most severe limits for socio-ecological explanations. In the paper the author has discussed two types of limits:

1. Limits due to incomparable or missing data. The author suggests that we would use theoretical models to bridge the gaps between the data one actually has and the one ought to have had.
2. Limits due to the faulty definition of units and missing connections among different levels of units.

The author further suggests that actor units must be included in order to construct links between different levels in a way furthering both the understanding of emergent properties and the understanding feedback effects. The distinction between actior units and non-actor units ars seen to facilitate the understanding of system dynamics at different levels.

Generally, decision makers do not reach across frontiers for ideas and experience, rather, when confronted with a problem to which it is politically expedient to react, they grasp at an ill-digested concept derived from elsewhere, often without appreciation of its origin and its effects. Various attempts have been made to systematise the identification of promising foreign ideas and their adoption at the local level. Alan Norton in his attempt outlines in his paper, "Policy analysis as a Starting Point for Comparative Studies," the conditions under which the international exchange of ideas or domestic policies can take place with the deepest possible understanding of their relevance and value in different national contents. In this paper the author deals with the utility of cross national comparative studies in the development of specific local policies and means by which their potential values may be realized. Practical experience of cross-national consultancies on policy problems and of the difficulties in communication is considered. The author finds that dissemination of policy ideas across national frontiers is a frequent occurrence but in general this happens without an understanding of the function performed by such ideas in the local context and their relationship to the social, cultural, economic and political environment in the country of origin sometimes at least without a sufficient appreciation of their likely effects and relationship to the different types of need in the countries which receive them. The author finds the need and asserts that a clearer appreciation is required of the contribution which foreign experience made and of the methodological approach from which the highest policy making benefits can be derived. The author assumes that such an approach must aim at a deep understanding of the environment of policies and affecting the process of implementation, both in the originating and in the receiving countries. The author shows an ardent desire for analytical approach through cross national partnerships of experts.

Since the late 1960s the process of structural economic change has considerably proceeded in those European countries with an industrial tradition reaching back to the late 18th and early 19th century. The major characteristics of this change are widely recognized, including changes in the industrial concentration, ownership patterns and geographical location and distribution of industrial enterprises. Klaus R. Kunzmann in his paper, "Structural Change in Old Industrial Agglomerations" deals with the process of structural economic change which has considerably proceeded in European countries which have a long industrial tradition. The author widely recognizes, the major characteristics of this change including changes in the industrial and occupational structure, the level of industrial concentration, ownership patterns and geographical location and distributing industrial enterprises. The author finds that these changes occured in the context of technological innovations, rationalization processes and changing social and cultural attitudes and aspirations, factors which are mutually independent. The author comes to the conclusion that the effects of structural economic changes have been felt most severely and generally in old industrial areas of North-West Europe which are based originally on the exploration of coal, on textile mills, on the production of iron and steel industries. The research projects identify, analyse and compare community and public authority responses to changing economic structure in old industrial areas using Merseyside in North-West England and the Rurgebiet in North-West Phalia as a reference area for empirical investigation. In this paper theoretical, methodological and organizational experiences from pilot study and from the on-going main research project are reported.

Many cross national comparative studies remove particular proceedings and policies from their specific national context in an often uncritical and idealistic way in order to use them as an invulnerable model to support the accomplishment of new strategies. Harald Bodenschatz, Volker Heise and Jochen Korf Macher analyse in their article, "Some Remarks to the Methodological Problems of International Comparative Studies on

Residents' Resistance in Urban Renewal." They suggest a methodological approach which, could avoid, this sort of criticism, has to meet the following requirements: The various proceedings and policies (as research issues) must be analysed in their local context (case studies); the national context in terms of relevant political and economic conditions influencing the local policies must be considered; the description of both levels—local and national—has to consist of the most important historical periods in order to cope with the variations and modifications of policies and proceedings during the process of their genesis and development.

The issue of whether cities in all Western societies are converging into a common path or urbanization has been a central question taken up in the "post-industrial" society debate. However such arguments ignore the fact that although there may exist similar patterns and problems, the origin of structures which have produced urban effects are different. David C. Thorns in his paper, "Comment on Topics of the Internationalization of Urban Problems: Comparing International Trends," adopts the approach that cities are the products of particular sets of social and economic conditions. It is customary that cities vary depending on where they are located. Australian and New Zeland cities are the reflection of the fact that in these societies the wealth base was initially pastoral production with a limited and small manufacturing base. According to the author cities in the cultural region were largely an amalgam of a service sector and a consumer oriented manufacturing sector. Attempts were made in 1970 and cities were being restructured as a result of the pursuit of primary products, export strategy which moves reserves to new settings and away upon the established urban centres. The author arrives at a conclusion that the categories of industrial and "post-industrial," of "convergence and "divergence" are misleading ones which divert attention from the real task of developing an accurate historically comparative analysis of urban development. The author forwards new direction by illustrating that it is only when there are studies available of the type that it will be possible to adequately assess the evidence of convergence or divergence in the path being followed or urban development within the different nation and States.

Cities perform many valuable functions for their national economies and resident populations. However, changing technological and industrial conditions (both nationally and internationally) cause these functions to change over time. In this regard it must be remembered that nearly all of the largest and most densely settled cities in America and Western Europe developed during a transportation and industrial era that no longer prevails. During this era cities possessed comparative advantages over other locations. John D. Kasarda in his paper, "New Urban Policies for New Urban Realities, postulates that modern advances in transportation, communications, and production technologies have transformed major Western cities from centres of material goods production into centres of administration and service provision. The author has visualized that this transformation has profoundly altered the traditional roles that larger, older cities performed as opportunity leaders for lesser educated, unskilled people. The author has arrived at a conclusion that growing entry-level job deficits now characterize their economy bases in contrast to the entry-level job surpluses that attracted and supported so many low-skill residents in the past. However, aided in part by well-intentioned Government subsidies, disadvantaged persons continue to be attracted and residentially anchored in inner city areas where there is little hope for their obtaining employment. The author is hopeful to visualize that revised urban policies should foster new service sector growth programmes created between cities and the disadvantage and facilities employmentre training and relocation of the urban structurally unemployed.

PART II: COMPARISON OF NATIONAL AND INTERNATIONAL URBAN RESEARCH

Comparative research is particularly fruitful when it is based upon research concepts and available findings on common topics concerning various countries. It is, therefore, of primary importance to compare the most perceived problems with the current research priorities in a number of countries. The most common problem perceived now a days in the European countries is undoubtedly that important changes in the economic srtucture as well as in the technologies used are taking place within the context of economic and sometimes of demographic stagnation. Jacques Robert in his paper, "Current Research Trends in the European Countries: Premises for Transnational and Comparative Urban and Regional Research," has made an attempt in this direction. He suggests that we should give primary importance to the need to compare the most perceived problem and current research priorities in a number of countries. The author finds that progressive alternatives of realistic planning alternatives induce a climate of uncertainty and anxiety in the field of urban and regional planning. He further comments that currently a number of economic and technological changes are under way and that not much can be done about their local and regional impacts, even when they are negative. The author enumerates the most pressing questions addressed to the urban and regional researchers as follows:

—What is the nature of the changes under way?
—What will be their impact at the regional and urban level?
—How far these changes are inevitable? Is it possible to reduce their negative impact? Is it possible to conceive alternative development strategies to counter balance the unfavourable effects of the changes underway?

Regarding these issues, the priorities in several European countries will be compared and selected research examples of national research will be discussed to prepare a catalogue which may be used as a starting point for the formulation of transnational and comparative research.

Horest M. Bolting, with the help of his paper titled as "Evaluating Urban and Regional Research in Federal Republic of Germany" surprises the reader with evaluating urban and regional research in the Federal Republic of Germany. The author has made an attempt to analyse the present significance of evaluation of research. He finds out the political applications of findings of evaluation research problems and has made an elaboration of future significance of evaluation research in the field of regional planning and urban development. In the end he himself concludes that the future significance of evaluation research in the field of regional planning and urban development depends on two forces: the pressure of demand and task involved and the resistance of those who might be affected by the measures. The author postulates that it is quite possible that the capacity of researchers to overcome the present methodological weakness will in the end decide whether the hope pinned on evaluation, research by many people will be fulfilled or whether it will become a theoretical field for individual researchers from whom the translation of findings in the policy is only of secondary importance.

Hellmut Wollmann, on the other hand, gives a nutshell report in the paper, "Trends in Urban Research in Germany," on the development of focus and of subject of (applied) urban research at German universities. He points out that comparatively swift changes in focus and orientation of urban research in Germany have come about within a few years.

Since the 1920's university researchers in France have devoted part of their research activities to urban phenomena. Particularly, the geographers have analysed the transition of France from a so far predominantly rural to an urbanized society. The fifth and sixth plans for economic and social development have led to the employment of research that was commissioned by the administrative agencies to mobilize all pertinent fields of research: engineering, building, economics and social sciences.

Jacques Parnelle in his brief article, "Urban Research in France," analyses the development of urban research in France, highlighting the availability of basic data and the development of research and institutions. The author has made an attempt to establish the identity of (i) the agencies for programming research, (ii) the agencies for conducting research and (iii) the discrimination of and promises of access to research.

Urban studies in Switzerland may be related to three major research traditions: urbanization—migration processes and urban ecology. Erwin Zimmerman in his brief article, "Urban Community Research in Switzerland" intends to provide some guidance to the relevant literature but has not attempted a systematic substative review.

According to the author Swiss urban research efforts in the past have been characterized by several limitations and the future is not bright. Recent fiscal and social problems in several Swiss cities have, however, created a more favourable national and political climate for urban research. The Swiss National Science Foundation plans to set up a special emphasis programme on urban problems. Financial assistance will stimulate researchers to take up the study of urban problems as without such financial assistance urban research in Switzerland would certainly remain an area of an occasional studies.

The time for recent investigation in the field of urban research was set by the urbanization report of the Dutch National Government in 1976. Henk Voogd in his brief article, "Urban Research in the Netherlands", provides an overview of some major urban issues in the Netherlands. It provides information about research institutions and agencies which are actively involved in urban research. The author feels, to avoid misunderstanding, this note does not claim to be complete.

Yugoslavia is a country with a relatively very low level of urban social research but at the same time there is a high rate of urbanization. Zdravko Mlinar in his paper, "Urban Social Research in Yugoslavia", provides a very short account of urban social research in Yugoslavia. According to him there are three characteristic approaches to the urban social research in Yugoslaiva: (i) literature which reflects (urban-rural) sociology and political sciences; (ii) the second is related to local politics and self-management within urban context; and (iii) the third characteristic approach to urban research indicates the most frequent studies which represent a response to the concrete, practical need of urban and spatial planning.

In Austria various institutions work in the field of urban research, e.g. Municipal Departments, Federal Ministries, State Governments, non-governmental agencies, private researchers and universities. Wolf Huber in his article, "Applied Urban Research in Austria", gives information about the various institutions working in the field of applied urban research. He also provides a critical assessment of applied urban research conducted in Austria.

The European coordination centre for research and documentation in social sciences (Vienna Centre) is an international non-governmental organization and an autonomous body of the international social science council. Armando Montainari in his paper, "Metropolitan Planning and Problems in Europe: The Contribution of Vienna Centre" reports the contribution of the Vienna Centre law and metropolitan planning and problems in Europe. It aims at facilitating scientific cooperation between social scientists from Eastern and Western Europe in all areas of social science. Its main activities are to coordinate cross national comparative research carried out by participants from Eastern and Western Europe, to organize conferences on topical social science, themes, to coordinate a programme of cooperation and change of social science information and documentation and to train social scientists in comparative research.

Hachiro Nakamura in his article, "The Bases of Urban Research in Japan," relates that about the beginning of the 1950s, when economic growth of Japan got underway, the growth of and interest in urban problems started. By the 1960s, when the densely inhabited districts had outgrown other areas, society became an urban one. Urban problems were sprouting and grew more seriously, and as a result an increasing number of professionals in the government, political circles, business, academic field have been paying attention to them. Recently sociology has made a serious effort to draw public attention to the need for the creation of community in the city.

REFERENCES

1. Daland, R.T., *Comparative Urban Research*, Sage Publications, I.N.C. London, 1969.
2. Walton, J. and Wasotti, L.H. (ed.), *The City in Comparative Perspective*, Sage Publications, New York, 1976.
3. Berry, B.J.L., *The Human Consequences of Urbanization*, New York, St. Maritius Press,

4. Germani, G. (ed), *Modernization, Urbanization and the Urban Crisis*, Boston, Little Brown, 1973.
5. Medows, P. and Migruehi, E.H. (ed), *Urbanism, Urbanization and Change; Comparative Perspectives*, Reading Mass Addision Wisely, 1969.
6. Fara, S.F. (ed), *Urbanism in World Perspective: Reader*, New York, Thomas; Little Brown, 1968.
7. Brease, G. (ed), *The City in Newly Developing Countries*, Engle Wood Cliffs N.J., Prentice Hall, 1969.
8. Clark, J.N., *Comparative Community Politics*, New York, Halsted Press (Sage Publications), 1974.
9. Tilly, C. (ed), *An Urban World*, Boston Little Brown, 1974.
10. Schwirian, K.P. (ed), *Comparative Urban Structure Studies in the Ecology of Cities*, Leington Mass. D.C., Heath, 1974.
11. Daland, R.T., 1969, *op. cit.*
12. Walton, J. and L.H. Wasotti, *op. cit.*
13. *Economic Geography*, 1971.
14. *The New Atlantic*
15. *Urban Affairs Quarterly*, 1972.
16. Daland, 1969, *op. cit.*
17. International Urban Research, Institute of International Studies, the *World's Metropolitan Atlas*, Berkely and Los Angeles University of California, 1959, pp. 1-2.
18. Walton, J., *Political Economy of World Urban Systems—Directions for Comparative Research in the City in Comparative Perspective.* Walton and Wasotti (ed), ch. 14, (1976).
19. Walton, Wasotti, 1976, *op. cit.*
20. Daland, R.T., 1969, *op. cit.*
21. Sears, R., Transcultural Variables and Conceptual Equivalence, in B. Kamplam (ed), *Study Personality Cross Culturally*, Evarston III, Row Peterson, 1961.
22. Przeworski, A. and Teune H., *The Logic of Comparative Social Inquiry*, New York, John Wiley, 1970.
23. Przewoski, 1970, *op. cit.*
24. Naroll, R., Some Thoughts on Comparative Method in Cultural Anthropology *in* H.M. Blalock and A. Blalock (eds), *Methodology in Social Research*, New York, McGrohill, 1968
25. Janet, Abu Lughod, "Legitimacy of Comparisons in Comparative Urban Studies: A Theoretical Position and an Application *to North African Cities, in The City in Comparative Perspective*, New York, Sage Publications, John Wiley and Sons.

SECTION ONE

LEARNING FROM COMPARATIVE URBAN RESEARCH

TWO

KARL-HEINZ SIMON AND BERND HAMM

SOME METHODOLOGICAL AND TECHNOLOGICAL ISSUES IN COMPARATIVE URBAN ANALYSIS

INTRODUCTION

CUS intends to investigate in the ecological structure of urban areas and to establish some relationships between urban differentiation and societal characteristics through a sample of nations (see CUS-Report No. 3). From a methodological point of view, urban differentiation will be studied in the traditions of social area analysis and factorial ecology. Furthermore special emphasis will be given to the elaboration of a more systematic comparative approach (see CUS-Report No. 2).

This paper discusses selected methodological and technical problems in comparative urban analysis. Some of these problems can only be approached by accepting certain assumptions. Additionally, not all of the made assumptions are methodologically sufficient enough to encompass the complex issues of comparative research. However, we hope that subsequent comments will help to clarify remaining methodological problems.

The scope and methods of comparative urban analysis

The objects of comparative urban analysis

The explanatory objective (or *universe*) of comparative urban ecology is the socio-spatial differentiation of a definite number of urban areas. Here, comparison may be either cross-sectional or longitudinal done for one or for more than one point in time. Socio-spatial differentiation is to be studied according to its dimensions, to the distribution of these dimensions in space, and to the intensity and tempo of change (Friedrichs 1978, p. 13). This means that the following prerequisites are needed for the conduct of comparative urban analysis:

1. A sample of urban areas
2. Variables to describe socio-spatial differentiation
3. Longitudinal data.

The purpose of comparative urban analysis is to demonstrate and examine

1. The differences and similarities in the socio-spatial structure of the urban areas
2. The direction and intensity of change in socio-spatial structure
3. The conditions of change, as a reflexion of societal characteristics.

The most general assumption that has to be accepted is that urban areas are not strictly idiosyncratic entities but are at least to some extent comparable in structure and development. If so, there must be certain regularities in urban development, even across different societies.

Comparative research may be defined as a strategy to examine whether or not a definite number of variables shows the same distribution values across at least two urban areas. The number of variables observed has to be definite, and any conclusion about whether the objects are similar or not can only refer to these variables.

Comparative analysis in urban ecology across different societies may be conducted to one or more of the following purposes:

1. Generalization of findings achieved by case studies. Are there, e.g., common factors of socio-spatial differentiation of urban areas not only in one society but in all societies included in the study?

2. Identification and explanation of differences in socio-spatial structure of urban areas in different societies. What are, e.g., the differences in factor patterns and how can these different patterns be explained?
3. Testing hypothesis on socio-spatial differentiation in a more systematic and rigorous manner. Is, e.g., the hypothesis that socio-economic, family and ethnic status will be extracted as common factors throughout the sample supported or fulsified?
4. Exploring the reciprocal effects between urban structure and societal characteristics—does, e.g., the importance of socio-economic status, family status, and ethnic status depend on a certain degree of societal development as described by variables related to the ecological complex?
5. Explorations into the dynamics of urban differentiation—e.g., is there, indeed, a time-lag in societal development and, *vice uersa*, does this time-lag affect urban structure?
6. Policy oriented research—e.g., if we find considerable similarities in urban differentiation for all the societies included, what would be the conclusions with respect to as far as urban development are concerned policies?

Classification of comparative urban analyses

How is CUS related to existing comparative urban analyses? If we classify existing comparative research according to

1. the number of urban areas included
2. the number of countries included
3. the number of points in time,

We arrive at the classification given in Table 2.1.

CUS, then, differs from other comparative approaches in attempting to include more than two urban areas from more than two societies and more than one point in time. CUS extends the complexity of comparison beyond the range of existing research.

It is especially this increase in complexity which causes some additional problems, both theoretical and methodological ones. The most crucial of these problems, with respect to

TABLE 2.1: Classification of comparative urban analysis (studies

Number of urban areas included	1	1	2	2
Number of countries included	1	1	1	1
Number of points in time	1	2 (and more)	1	2 (and more)
		I	II	III
Type of Study	Case Study	Case Study, Longitudinal	Intra-Societal/ Internatio-nal Compa-rison, Pairwise Cross- sectionl	Intra-Societal Internatio-nal Com-parison, Pairwise, Cross-sectional and Longi-tudinal
Examples of studies	Sweetser, 1961 Sweetser 1965, Bell 1955 Janson 1968 Abu-Lughod 1969, Bahr 1978, Berry: Rees 1969, Hamm 1977, Hamm 1979, Jones 1969, Gronholm 1969 Shevky/Bell 1955	Hunter 1971, Hunter 1974, Brown/Horton 1970 Hunter/Latif 1973 Murdie 1969 Weclawowicz 1979 Timms 1970 C.P. LO 1975, McElrath 1980	Kaufman 1961 Pitts 1971	Dent 1972 Latif 1974

in factorial ecology and social area analysis)

2	2	3 (and more)	3 (and more)	3 (and more)	3 (and more)
2	2	1	1	2 (and more)	2 (and more)
1	2 (and more)	1	2 (and more)	1	2 (and more)
IV	V	VI	VII	VIII	IX
Inter-Societal/ International Comparison, Pairwise Cross-sectional	Inter-Societal/ International Comparison, Pairwise Cross-sectional and Longitudinal	Intra-Societal/ International Comparison, Cross-sectional	Intra-Societal/ International Comparison, Cross-sectional, and Longitudinal	Intra-Societal/ International Comparison, Cross-sectional	Intra-Societal/ International Comparison, Cross-Sectional and Longitudinal
Sweetser 1965, Sweetser 1969 Clignet/ Sween 1969		Schwirian/ Matre 1974, Timms 1970, Schmid 1950, Van Arsdol/ Camiller/ Schmid 1959	Salins 1971, Berry/ Spodek 1971	Schwirian/ Smith 1974	CUS

empirical analysis, consists in the availability of a comparable data base, cross-sectional as well as longitudinal.

Levels of analysis and units of observation

CUS includes three levels of analysis:

1. Societies
2. Urban areas
3. Census tracts

The second unit, urban areas, and its internal structure is our prime interest, and therefore the ultimate dependent construct. Nations serve as contextual units in the explanation of urban structure i.e. they constitute in-dependent constructs. Census tracts are the units of observation, they give the data base without being, in themselves, in the focus of interest. So What we intend to conduct is a two-or three? level—or contextual, analysis. At no point in the analysis we will use individual, or behavioural arguments. The line of reasoning is on a strictly aggregate basis and we explore in context effects in a descriptive, correlational way. This characteristic may serve as a distinction between CUS and the study of metropolitan development currently conducted at the University of Hamburg (Friedrichs *et al.* 1981). On each the three levels of analysis, however, we face the problem of statistical delimitation. There is no definition of census tracts or urban areas common to all the societies (which, in itself poses a problem of definition) or all urban areas to be included. To tackle this problem, several decisions have to be made:

1. The only way to define "society" as the context unit is to equal "society" with "nation." Even if this may not be accepted without deeper discussion, we have to rely on statistical data prepared for nations as they are reported by UN, World Bank and other sources (see CUS-Report No. 3).
2. There is no definition of "urban area" generally accepted for all the nations (Hawley 1971, among others, discusses this problem). Even if we only intend to analyse urban

areas with more than 100.000 inhabitants, we have to decide between "urban area" and "city proper." Neither one nor the other are defined in a satisfyable and comparable way (according to the terms used by Berry 1972, we have overbounded and underbounded urban areas). One way to solve this problem might be to accept the delimitation of metropolitan areas proposed by Davis 1959. But, as there are no census tract reports available for these units, this would be of little help for the purpose of CUS. The only common denominator is the city proper, here we find census tract data for all nations. If we want to take into account suburbanization, we only can determine an index of suburbanization (Kasarda 1972) as one of the variables describing urban structure.

3. Definitions of census tracts differ highly within and between nations. For some cities, block data are available for others urban sub-units may have 10.000 or even more inhabitants. As the values of correlation coefficients (as well as of, e.g. segregation and dissimilarity indices) depend on the number of cases observed, we have to define units which are common throughout all of the cities. The most comprehensive data sets are available from the census of the United States; however, our attempt to conduct more systematic comparative research may usefully be contrasted against earlier studies most of which have been done in U.S. cities. It is suggested by these arguments that we take the census tract of the U.S. census reports as the standard unit, i.e., units with populations of approximately 4000 to 6000 inhabitants. Consequently, in the case where block data are available, we have to aggregate them to approach the size of the standard unit (in this case, an aggregation rule must be found); but in the case of cities with sub-units considerably greater than the standard unit, disaggregation is not possible. As a consequence, the city has to be substituted by another one with appropriate sub-units.

The homogeneity-heterogeneity problem in ecological analysis has been discussed for several decades (Jahn, Schmid, Schrag

1947) but never, to our knowledge, adequately been solved. Its relevance for analyses in factorial ecology has not yet been systematically proved. We may propose some tests within the context of CUS; however, at this preliminary stage, a pre-definition and optimal approximation of the standard unit has to be achieved. From a theoretical point of view, heterogeneity might be an effect of structure (segregation might be more small scale in smaller cities) or an effect of process (succession causes heterogeneity, e.g.). It seems useful, then, to characterize census tracts by an index of heterogeneity and to look for interpretation of the spatial arrangement of tracts with different values on the index.

For each of the definitions mentioned—nation, city proper, and census tract—our analyses will necessarily suffer from inadequacies of the data sources. It is, in the course of CUS, impossible to overcome these shortcomings. The demand for comparability poses severe restrictions on the available data basis. We have to be well aware of this problem without, however, being able to propose a satisfying solution.

Dimensions of urban differentiation and selection of indicators

CUS intends to explore the socio-spatial differentiation, or ecological structure of cities. What, then, is socio-spatial differentiation? What are its dimensions? What are the indicators to measure it in quantitative terms? Starting from an understanding of the construct which is near to common sense, multidimensional analysis is necessary to answer these questions. But in doing so, we have to take into account that, in principal, socio-spatial differentiation is an extremely complex phenomenon. Whatever the dimensions (or the indicators related to them) of the analysis, additional ones are conceivable. The number of dimensions (and indicators) is unlimited, indefinite. From an indefinite universe we have to select "important" dimensions (and indicators). The problem of content validity cannot exactly be solved.

On what grounds may the problem be approached? The deductive way to do dimensional analysis starts from a theory of urban differentiation and development. The core of the argument has been outlined in CUS-Report No. 2 as the Generalized-Burgess-Model. The inductive way has been followed by factorial ecologists since the first introduction of social area analysis (Bell 1955). An overview over substantive findings of the factorial ecology tradition is also given in CUS-Report No. 2. As a synthesis of these two approaches, the following dimensions of urban differentiation are hypothesized as important ones:

1. Specialization of land use
2. Segregation according to socio-economic status
3. Segregation according to family status
4. Segregation according to ethnicity
5. Migration
6. Density

These dimensions seem to be fairly general, at least for urban areas in highly industrialized capitalist societies. They are, however, still abstract constructs which have to be translated if we want to measure them in quantitative form. What we need, then, are indicators to define the six dimensions.

Here again, the number of indicators describing each dimension is potentially unlimited. There are no criteria to check for content validity. On the other hand, as the variables describing each dimension are highly intercorrelated, we only need relatively few indicators to account for a sufficiently large amount of information (Hamm 1978, 1979): The indicators, we would like to analyse, include:

—land values, work places, day-time-population, office space, service space, median number of floors, ecological distance (for specialization of land use);
—income, rent, education, blue collar workers, unskilled workers, MPO-ratio, owner occupied housing units (for class segregation);
—sex ratio, fertility, singles, persons per household, age, women in the labour force, dependency ratio (for family status);
—immigration, emigration, lengths of residence (for migration);

—foreign stock, ethnic minorities (for ethnic segregation);
—persons per housing unit, persons per room, persons per structure, persons per acre (for density).

These indicators are supposed to represent our six dimensions and, at the same time define in measurable terms the general construct of socio-spatial differentiation.

For purposes of comparison, we need to have data for all these indicators from all census tracts of all cities in the sample, for all nations to be included, and for more than one time point. These data requirements are by no means fulfilled. The real data situation poses severe restrictions on the analysis not only for reasons of availability but also for reasons of comparability: Does income describe the same aspect of socio-economic status in Poland as in the U.S.? Do land values play the same role for specialization of land use in socialist as in capitalist societies? Does 'persons per acre' mean the same in the Netherlands as in Norway? Even if we had available all the data we needed, there would be no shortcut answer to questions like these. The problem of content comparability turns out to be the most crucial difficulty in our research. At the moment, we can only admit that we have no satisfying solution, at hand.

We will attempt to find a fairly common set of variables for all our dependent units, and to start with our analyses on these grounds. If we expose our attempts to scholarly discussion, new and better solutions may be found.

With respect to the quality of our data base, we have to rely on the sources from which data are made available. In general, we are restricted to make use of official census material, with only rare chances for supplementation. This means, of course, that CUS analyses will necessarily suffer from all the shortcomings inherent in census data. There is no possibility for correction. This is equally true for shortcomings in data collection as well as for the redefinition of variables or for changes in the units of observation between two or more points in time. If there are—and there certainly are—measurement errors, it is not possible to decide whether they are systematic or stochastic in nature and what might be artificial outcomes and analytical results.

Selection and use of statistical techniques

A great variety of statistical methods and techniques for urban analysis have been developed by social ecology, regional sciences, quantitative geography, and other disciplines. This section does not intend to deal with all of them but only with those which seem, at the present state of reflection, most appropriate to assist in the description of urban structure.

Most of our variables will be expressed as percentages, and we shall treat percentages as interval measures. The first group of statistical techniques we intend to use is simply measures of centrality and variability (mean, standard deviation, coefficients of variation, range). This group needs on further discussion, although many case studies have failed to report these measures which are necessary for adequate interpretation.

The second group of techniques contains multivariate statistics: factor analysis, cluster analysis, multiple regression, canonical correlation. All of them, except cluster analysis, are based on the logic of correlation, and require continuity and linearity of bivariate distributions. In earlier work (Hunter and Latif 1973, Hamm 1979) it had been shown that different factor models do not produce substantially different factor patterns. So it may be legitimate to only select principal components and principal axes models (the latter might be replaced by Rao's canonical factor analysis). Multiple regression and canonical correlation will be used to explore the contextual impact of the societal on the local level. Cluster analysis might help to solve the problem of aggregating small units of observation and to approximate the standard census tract unit. It may also be useful to determine spatial patterns in the distribution of indicators or indices. Computer software packages employed are SPSS and CLUSTAN.

A third group of techniques includes social area analysis, index construction, and gradient analysis. Gradient analysis requires ecological distance-measures which will hardly be available in our data sets. In one case or the other ecological distance might be substituted by linear distance, but this cannot allow for adequate tests of the Burgers model (Quinn 1940). Social area analysis is a potentially powerful technique, provided that indicators are soundly based in ecological theory (see CUS-Report No. 2). Its usefulness has by no means been exhausted in published research, and we expect to demonstrate some new applications in comparative and dynamic analyses. Index construction will be very important in CUS, because we shall attempt to give summary measures for socio-spatial differentiation of entire urban areas. Indices as those proposed by Duncan (1955), by Gibbs and Martin (1959), or other authors will be carefully examined for application to other variables. These and other indices have received elaborate attention within the last years. The methodological results and insights of this previous work will be very usefull in our own research.

REFERENCES

Abu-Lughod, J.L., Testing the Theory of Social Area Analysis: The Ecology of Cairo, Egypt. *American Sociological Review* 34, 198-212, 1969.

Arsdol, M.V., Camilleri, S.F., Schmid, C.F., The Generality of Urban Social Area Indexes, *American Sociological Review* 23, 277-284, 1958.

Bahr, J., Santiago de Chile: Eine Faktorenanalytische Untersuchung zur inneren Differenzierung einer lateinamerikanischen Millionenstadt. *Mannheimer Geographische Arbeiten* 4, 1978.

Bell, W., Economic, Family and Ethnic Status: An Empirical Test, *American Sociological Review*, 20, 45-52, 1955.

Berry, B.J.L. (ed.), Comparative Factorial Ecology. *Economic Geography*, 47, Supplement 2, 1971.

Berry, B.J.L., Smith, K.B. (eds.), *City Classification Handbook*. New York, 1972.

Berry, B.J.L., Rees, P.H., The Factorial Ecology of Calcutta. *American Journal of Sociology* 74, 445-491, 1969.

Berry, B.J.L., Szodek, H., Comparative Ecologies of Large Indian Cities. *Economic Geography* 47, 266-285, 1971.

Brown, L.A., Horton, F.E., Social Area Change: An Empirical Analysis, *Urban Studies* 7, 271-288, 1970.

Clignet, R., Sween, J., Accra and Abidjan: A Comparative Examination of the Theory of Increase in Scale. *Urban Affairs* 4, 297-324, 1969.

Davis, K. *The World's Metropolitan Areas*. Berkeley and Los Angeles, 1959.

Dent, O.F., "Aspects of Change in Urban Social-Spatial Structure." Unpublished Ph. D. dissertation, Ann Arbor, 1955.

Duncan, O.D., Duncan, B., Residential Distribution and Occupational Stratification. *American Journal of Sociology* 60, 493-503, 1955.

Friedrichs, J. (Hg.), Stadtentwicklungen in kapitalistischen und sozialistischen Londern, *Reinbek bei Hamburg*, 1978.

Friedrichs, J., Einige Probleme vergleichender Stadtforsuchung. Arbeitspapier fur die Sektion "Stadt-und Regionalsoziologie" *zur Sitzung am* 8.-10.4.1981 in Arnoldshain, 1981.

Gibbs, J.P., Martin, W.T., Toward a Theoretical System of Human Ecology. *Pacific Sociologica Review* 2, 29-36, 1959.

Gronholm, L., The Ecology of Social Disorganization in Helsinki. *Acta Sociologica* 5, 31-41, 1961.

Hamm, B., Die Organisation der stadtischen Umwelt. Ein Beitrag zur sozialokologischen Theorie der Stadt. Frauenfeld und Stuttgart, 1977.

Hamm, B., "Land Use and Segregation. Paper presented to the 9th World Congress of Sociology." Uppsala dt. in: Hamm, B. (Hg.) (1979): *Lebensraum Stadt*. Beitrage zur Sozialokogie deutscher Stadte. Frankfurt, S. 181-200, 1978.

Hamm, B. *Indikatoren der Stadtentwicklung*, Trierer Beitrage zur Stadt- und Regionalplanung Bd. 3. Trier 1979.

Hawley. A.H., *Urban Society: An Ecological Approach*, New York, 1971.

Hunter, A., The Ecology of Chichgo: Persistence and Change, 1930-1960. *American Journal of Sociology* 77, 425-444, 1971

Hunter, A., Community Change: A Stochastic Analysis of Chicago's Local Communities, 1930-1960, *American Journal of Sociology* 79, 923-947, 1974.

Hunter, A., Latif, A.H., Stability and Change in the Ecological Structure of Winnipeg: A Multi-Method Approach. *Canadian Review of Sociology and Anthropology* 10, 308-333, 1973.

Jahn, J., Schmid, C.F., Schrag, C., The Measurement of Ecological Segregation. *American Sociological Review* 12, 293-303, 1947.

Janson, C.G., The Spatial Structure of Newyork, New Jersey, Part 1: The Central City. *Acta Sociologica* 11, 144-169, 1968.

Jones, F.L., *Dimensions of Urban Social Structure: The Social Areas of Melbourne*, Australia. Toronto, 1969.

Kasarda, J.D., "The Theory of Ecological Expansion," *Social Forces* 51, 1972.

Kaufmann, W.C., Social Area Analysis: An Explication of Theory, Methodology and Techniques, with Statistical Tests of Revised Procedures, San Francisco and Chicago. 1950. Evaston III, (unpublished Ph. D. Dissertation. Northwestern University), 1961.

Latif, A.H., "Factor Structure and Change Analysis of Alexandria", Egypt, 1947 and 1960. in: Schwirian, K.P. (ed.), *Comparative Urban Structure*. Lexington 338-349, 1974.

LO, C.P., Changes in the Ecological Structure of Hong Kong 1961-1971:

A Comparative Analysis. *Environment and Planning* A 7, 941-963, 1975.

McElrath, D.C., "Changing Social Differentiation of Rome: 1951-1971." Unpublished dr .ft, 1980.

Murdie, R.A., "The Factorial Ecology of Metropolitan Toronto, 1951-1961. An Essy of the Social Geography of the City. Chicago, 1969.

Pitts, F.R., "Factorial Ecology of Seoul and Taegu, Korea: A Preliminary Report." *Economic Geography* 47, 300-302, 1971.

Quinn, A., "Burgess Zonal Hypothesis and its Critics" *American Sociological Review* 5, 713-722, 1940.

Salins, P.D., "Household Location Patterns in American Metropolitan Areas." *Economic Geography* 47, 234-248, 1971.

Schmid, C.F., Generalizations concerning the Ecology of the American City. *American Sociological Review* 15, 264-281, 1950.

Schwirian, K.P., "Smith, R.K., Primacy, Modernization and Urban Structure: The Ecology of Puerto Rican Cities." in: Schwirian, K.P. (ed.), *Comparative Urban Structure*, Lexington, 324-338, 1974.

Schwirian, K.P., Matre, M., The Ecological Structure of Canadian Cities in: Schwirian, K.P. (ed.): *Comparative Urban Structure*. Lexington, 309-324, 1974.

Shevky, E., Bell, W., "Social Area Analysis. Theory, Illustrative Applications and Computational Procedures." Stanford, Calif, 1955.

Sweetser, F.L., *Social Ecology of Metropolitan Boston: 1950*, Boston, 1961.

Sweetser, F.L., "Factor Structure as Ecological Structure in Helsinki and Boston." *Acta Sociologica* 8, 205-225, 1965.

Sweetser, F.L., Factorial Ecology: Helsinki 1960. *Demography* 2, 372-385, 1965.

Sweetser, F.L., "Ecological Factors in Metropolitan Zones and Sectors." in, Dogan, M., Rokkan, S. (eds.), *Quantitative Ecological Analysis in the Social Sciences*, Cambridge, Mass, 1969.

Timms, D.W.G., "Comparative Factorial Ecology: Some New Zealand Examples." *Environment and Planning* 2, 455-467, 1970.

Timms, D.W.G., The Urban Mosaic: Toward a Theory of Residential Differentiation. Cambridge, London, New York, Melbourne, 1971.

Weclawowocz, G., "The Structure of Socio-Economic Space in Warsaw, 1931 and 1970." in: French, R.A., Hamilton, F.E. (eds.): *The Socialist City*. Chichester, 1979.

THREE

BURKHARD HOFMEISTER

CROSS-CULTURAL STUDIES ON URBAN STRUCTURE
Research Goals, Historical Development, Results, Current Problems

THREE SCALES FOR RESEARCH ON URBAN STRUCTURE

THERE are different points of view from which to look at urban structure. One point of view emphasizes the peculiarities of each individual city stressing the specific features and the *uniqueness of each city* as to its location, origin, historical development, morphology, functions, be they basic or non-basic, and its structure. It is obvious that this opinion is especially held by urban historians who are inclined to elaborate the historical events applicable to just the one city in question. No pair of cities are completely alike so that only a monograph on a single city can do justice to its personality.

In contrast, a different point of view emphasizes those features which may be labeled as truely urban in a sense that they are apt to characterize *every city in the world* at least during a certain period of time. Every city got certain forms and performs certain functions; it got some sort of a street pattern and building fabric, however different these may be from one place to the other; and it performs some functions, especially service functions and, in most cases, also some functions related to the secondary or the production sector of the economy. It is also obvious that this opinion, which is completely different from the one mentioned first, is especially held by urban economists who are eager to find out about all urban features which may be explained and even measured by general rules.

In a recent paper Holzner pointed out that this line was mainly followed by American geographers during the first two post-war decades. "Tempted by the common euphoria of the 1950s and 1960s which was the era of hard science in America, geographers believed that urban phenomena could be studied in basically the same way as phenomena in the natural sciences and that the scientific approach and methodological procedures of the natural sciences could be adapted directly to urban geography. It was also hoped that this approach could help to overcome the lack of respectability (among the other social sciences) of human geography in general and of urban geography in particular. This has indeed led to some spectacular success. It has, on the other hand, made urban geography too abstract and general, because it has taken much of the 'geography' out of the discipline, since most if not all of the cultural-genetic variations of cities throughout the world had to be 'purposely sacrified' in order to arrive at general similarities, regularities, and order in urban spatial structure" (Holzner 1981, p. 174).

It is, indeed, not too difficult a task to gather arguments in favour of both points of view and thus to justify either one. Both the individual scale and the global scale are applicable to the study of urban geography. However, even if either approach is being used this will not do full justice to the complete understanding of urban phenomena.

Somewhere in between those two extremes—one single city as an individual on the one side, all cities throughout the world as a kind or species on the other side—there is a median scale as an alternative view. The goal is to look at *a group of cities in a particular region* exhibiting a limited number of features making them similar to each other, but, at the same time, different from the cities in other regions. There are features inherent in any particular region: ideas and thoughts of their inhabitants and the desire of people to create their settlements accordingly. Cities are, to a certain degree, a mirror of the intentions of their founding fathers and their inhabitants over the centuries.

To give just one example, in Germany evidence has proved urban houses especially in the old town kernels to resemble the houses of the town's rural hinterland. The use of particular building materials of local origin, of respective building styles best adapted to those materials, the application of particular ground plans of houses as well as angles of houses in relation to the direction of the street derived from their respective rural prototypes give the towns their *regional imprint.* Huttenlocher in applying such criteria to the towns of South Germany came up with several urban regions (Huttenlocher 1963) while Scholler in an earlier paper stressed the socalled "tribal affiliation" (in terms of the old Germanic tribes of the early Middle Ages) of Germany's urban places (Scholler 1957).

In order to appropriately evaluate those features common to the cities in a particular region one got to search for the ideas behind the observable pattern of urban places. In many cases in these are cosmological, geomantic, or religious ideas deeply rooted the thinking of peoples or the inhabitants of a particular culture region, ideas that have been kept alive over the centuries and that have predetermined all details of the site and the original layout of the cities of their sphere of influence.

THE DEVELOPMENT OF THE CULTURAL-GENETIC APPROACH

The study of such regionally defined groups of cities has a tradition of almost a century although this aspect has long been neglected and only recently gained greater consideration and reputation. As early as 1885 the German author F.G. Hahn published a paper on "The cities of the North German plain and their relation to the area's physiography" (Hahn 1885). But there was still a long way to go before the first cross-cultural study of cities would appear. Probably the oldest study of the kind in the German geographical literature was a comparative study on the American and European cities by the Vietnamese geographer Oberhummer in 1915 who three years earlier had participated in the American Transcontinental excursion and contributed to the memorial volume of the excursion. Five years later Fleure in England published a paper on the cities in various ports of Europe in the journal Geographical Review (Oberhummer 1915, Fleure 1920).

The first attempt toward a comprehensive cross-cultural study of cities throughout the world was a symposium under the leadership of S. Passarge who, as a result of this meeting, edited a volume *Stadtlandschaften der Erde* (Urban landscapes of the world) in 1930 (Passarge 1930). From the viewpoint of the history of urban geography it is interesting to realize that this publication did not initiate any further research along those lines. This was only the beginning of the functional phase of urban geography in Germany and other European countries, and the foundation laid by Passarge and his co-authors was not worked upon prior to the second post-war decade.

The general textbook on "Urban Geography" by Beaujeu-Garnier and Chabot first published in France in 1963 was the first and, for a considerable period of time, was to remain the only textbook on urban geography to recognize this approach and to devote a lengthy chapter to the elaboration of the peculiar features of the cities in different parts of the world.

The present writer also devoted a chapter of his book on urban geography to the cultural-genetic approach (Hofmeister 1969, 4th ed. 1980), but so far there are quite a few textbooks on urban geography by American authors omitting this aspect altogether. Thus Holzner still has good reason to complain of this deficiency (Holzner 1981). On the other hand there are now lots of papers on the cities of some particular region of the world, and a considerable portion of Scargill's recent book *The form of cities* is devoted to the cultural-genetic approach and to models of regional types of cities throughout the world (Scargill 1979).

THE SPATIAL FRAME OF REFERENCE FOR THE CULTURAL-GENETIC APPROACH

One starting point for studies of urban structures has been the statement that there exists a median scale between the two extremes of treating each city as an individual and searching for common features of the cities in a world-wide context. Just what should the spatial frame of reference be on a median scale between the two extremes?

There are, no doubt, several possibilities depending on the respective aim of research. One may, of course, make an investigation of the urban places in the hinterland of a metropolis or of a series of urban places along some natural or cultural line such as the seaports along some shoreline, the cities of the fall-line separating the Appalachian Piedmont from the coastal plain or the cities along an escarpment, along a railway line or an historical boundary line. One may also carry out research on the urban places of any historical region such as the cities of a former German province, on the cities of any particular state or of a certain group of states or, finally, the cities of a whole continent, or even better, of those of a great culture region.

It was the German geographer Kolb who in two interesting papers developed the concept of the culture continent (Kulturerdteil). Within the inhabited portion of the world he distinguished between *ten* such culture regions of continental scope: the Occidental, the Russian, the Near Eastern (or Islamic), the Indian, the Sino—(or Chinese), the Indonese-Pacific, the Australian-Pacific, the Black African, the Angloamerican, and the Latinamerican culture regions (Kolb 1962, 1966).

In their textbook on urban geography mentioned above Beaujeu Garnier and Chabot derived at *fourteen* culture regions. In comparison with Kolb's concept these authors devided the occidental culture region into four subregions: Northern Europe, Central and Western Europe, Mediterranean Europe, and Eastern Europe. This breakdown, however, means a more detailed investigation on a lower level which, on the other hand, is only applied to the European continent. Since this procedure does not seem to be really justified we should reduce the various portions of Europe to the one occidental culture region of Kolb's concept and shall thus derive at *eleven* culture regions.

Holzner in his paper on "World regions in urban geography" (Holzner 1967) derives at 34 sub-regions which are then aggregated to *twelve* major world regions or, if we do not consider Isreal a major region in contrast to Holzner, also *eleven* as in the case of Beaujeu-Garnier and Chabot. Although his regions are defined in a somewhat different way we may as well take them as culture regions in terms of Kolb's concept. In Holzner's own words:

> The proposed regional system in urban geography is based upon the areal variation of processes that functionally associate cities and cultures. . . .Therefore, the habitable world is divided into regions on the basis of the variation of the above mentioned seven complexes of processes that associate cities and cultures: the processes of mutual historical influence, the processes of mutual economic relations, the processes of mutual technological relations, the processes of mutual population relations, the processes of mutual religious-philosophical influence, the processes of mutual ethnic relations, the processes of mutual socio-political relations. . . . However, since these processes functionally associate cultures and cities, it is to be expected that the various aspects of the cities in a given region reveal certain cultural-genetic characteristics (Holzner 1967, pp. 708 and 710).

In the volume *Japanese cities* edited by the Association of Japanese Geographers in 1970 a Paper by Masai was included who from a Far-Eastern point of view tried to look at his own country's urban places within a cross-cultural context. In this paper he distinguished between *nine* tonwscapes: It is interesting to learn that he made a distinction between the European cities and the Mediterranean cities, but considered the Russian cities to be of European origin. The Islamic and Indian culture regions were subsumed under the heading "Afrasian", the Japanese and Southeast Asian culture regions under the heading "Pacific Asian." In the New World he identified, aside of the Angloamerican and the Latinamerican culture regions, the "Amerindian" townscape as a district type.

The present writer in his recent book on urban structures (Hofmeister 1980) distinguished between *twelve* culture regions. In order to make easier a comparison of the various regionalizations mentioned above the following table has been compiled.

Culture regions or cultural-genetic urban types according to

Kolb 1962	Beaujeu-Garnier and Chabot 1963	Holzner 1967	Masai 1970	Hofmeister 1980
Occidental	Northern Europe Central/Western Europe Mediterranean Europe Eastern Europe	Europe	Europe Mediterranean	Europe
Russian	Traditional Russia Soviet Asia	Soviet Union		Russia/Soviet Union
Near Eastern	Near East North Africa	Near East Israel	Afrasian	Near East
Indian	South/Southeast Asia	South Asia		India
Sino	Far East	East Asia Japan	East Asia	China Japan
Indonese-Pacific			Pacific Asian	Southeast Asia
Australian-Pacific	Australia/New Zealand	Australia/New Zealand		Australia/New Zealand
Black African	Africa South of Sahara	Central and South Africa	Black African	Tropical-Africa South Africa
Anglo-american	America North of Rio Grande	Anglo-american	Anglo-american Amerindian	Anglo-american
Latin-american	America South of Rio Grande	Latin-american	Latin-american	Latin-american

MODELS OF CULTURAL-GENETIC TYPES OF CITIES

This far-reaching agreement of urban geographers on the concept of culture regions and their confines is reflected in the models or idealized plans developed for each of them, with only two exceptions. These models cannot possibly be discussed here in any detail, but it may be useful to have a list of the existing models for the purpose of reference.

The most comprehensive set of models of cultural-genetic types of cities was prepared by Knubel (1978). His models are, however, rather simple sketches and mainly destined for use in the classrooms of secondary schools in urban geography teaching. Quite a number of models is presented in Scargill's book (1979). There are models for the European city of Lichtenberger (1970, 1972), for the Russian city (particularly the medium-sized city of the Soviet era) by Mellor (1976), for the Islamic city by Dettmann (1969) and Seger (1975) and, with special regard to peculiar developments in various parts of the Near East and to the westernized type represented by such a cosmopolitan city as Istanbul, by Koch (1977), Lawless (1976), and Leitner (1981), for the Indian city by Caralp (1972) and Smailes (1969), for the Southeast Asian port city by McGee (1967), for the South African city by Davies (1972), a model which was adopted by Johnston in his recent bok "City and Society" (1980), by Schneider/Wiese (in Klimm/Schneider/Wiese 1980), and by Hofmeister (1982), for the Angloamerican city by Boskoff (1970), Holzner (1972), and Watson (1979), for the Latinamerican city by Bahr (1976), Borsdorf (1978), Griffin and Ford (1980), Bahr and Mertins (1981) and, presented as a time-space profile of dynamic change, by Gormsen (1981), for the Australian city with special reference to the metropolitan development of Sydney and Melbourne by Burnley (1976, 1980), and for the Japanese city with special regard to the castle town by Tanabe (1970) and Gutschow (1974).

CONTROVERSIES IN CROSS-CULTURAL STUDIES OF URBAN STRUCTURE

There are certain difficulties involved in applying the concept of the culture region to the elaboration of cultural-genetic types of cities. They become especially obvious while dealing with developments *limited to particular epochs* or eras on one hand and concerning *more than one culture region* on the other hand. Such phenomena are the colonial city of the 19th century and the socialist city of the 20th century.

Since the turn of the 16th century, but at an accelerated rate during the 19th century, large areas of Africa, South and Southeast Asia came under the rules of European peoples. The Europeans founded settlements of their own like the cantonments in India near existing indigenous cities. Such settlements usually had a grid-iron pattern, particular building styles like the bungalow developed in India and introduced to other areas of colonial occupancy, and separated from the city of the indigenous population by a cordon sanitaire. Thus the *colonial city* cannot be regarded a development of the cities of the respective countries, but was only incorporated into the growing metropolises during a later stage in the 20th century. If we consider *time* only, the colonial city may be compared with the industrial city in Western European countries or the United States of America. As soon as we consider the *spatial development* we got to realize that the colonial city was a phenomenon *beside* the development of the city indigenous to the respective culture region.

The second phenomenon to be considered here is the socalled *socialist city*. Some cities in the socialist countries are New Towns explicitly founded in underdeveloped parts of those countries in order to promote the manufacturing industry as a base of the regional economy. But aside from those newly founded cities transformations have been carried out in the older existing cities while transferring particular political ideas to architecture and town planning. Major aspects have been the design of the city centre including a huge square for parades and a main thoroughfare (Magistrale), an idea which was abandoned in recent years, the culture palace, the culture park etc. Private ownership of urban land was abolished thus eliminating the competition of various functions for central locations so characteristic for Western cities. Models of the socialist city have been published by Dawson in 1971 (see also Scargill 1979) and by Hamilton (in French/Hamilton 1979).

There are, however, symptoms of a convergence of city forms and structures in socialist and non-socialist countries.

> If this conclusion is correct, time, the increasing willingness of Western societies to exert some control over urban development, and the common adoption of improved methods of transport, traffic control, building and planning in countries of different social philosophy will work to diminish many of the present contrasts in city form (Dawson 1971, p. 112).

Thus, the development of the socialist city, although not yet terminated like the epoch of the colonial city, is very likely to merge with the modern universal trends of urbanization and may, just as well as the colonial city, be subsumed under the global concept of the culture regions.

The final question to be discussed is the controversial issue of whether the urbanization processes and their resulting urban structures are working on a world-wide scale *dependently or independently on culture*. In other words: Are there universal processes of urbanization making for convergences toward similar urban structures throughout the World? Or are there different processes of urbanization in the various culture regions making for different urban structures in each region? Or are there universal processes which are subject to modifications in each culture region thus producing different urban structures?

For a long time the idea of universal processes of urbanization had been maintained. During the 1970s, however, Berry among others deviated from this opinion by pointing out in his book *The human consequences of urbanization* (Berry 1973) that there are fundamentally different processes of urbanization at work depending on the different socio-political contexts represented by the United States with her pluralistic society, the Western Eropean walfare states, the countries of the Third World with autocratic regimes in many of them, and the socialist countries with their planned state economy.

Among the greatest critics of this opinion was Harvey with

his review of Berry's book in the 1975 volume of the *Annals of the Association of American Geographers.* Also Jones who on behalf of the IGU Commission on Processes and Patterns of Urbanisation edited a book *Essays on World Urbanization* (Jones 1975) represented the traditional opinion. In the more recent volume edited by Berry in 1976 on "Urbanization and counter-urbanization" he somewhat swang to the traditional opinion although in Berry/Kasarda's book of 1977 "*Contemporary Urban Ecology*" the differences were again stressed in a comparative chapter on urban developments in the United States, the United Kingdom, and the Soviet Union each representing three of the groups mentioned above. The present writer is of the opinion that there is sufficient evidence for supporting the third alternative: the processes are universal, but the several cultures make for different results, i.e. different urban structures in the various culture regions of the world.

CONCLUSION

Somewhere between the idiographic view of the individual city and the positivist search for general rules applicable to the development and structure of all cities throughout the world there is a median scale of looking at groups of cities, e.g. those cities located in a distinct culture region.

As it was shown there is a far-reaching agreement among urban geographers working along these lines in various countries such as Holzner in the United States, Beaujeu-Garnier and Chabot in France, Kolb and the present writer in Germany as to the existence of approximately a dozen such culture regions and, accordingly, a dozen cultural-genetic types of urban structure in the world.

In each of these culture regions the processes of urbanization which are more or less the same throughout the world encounter different traditions and different societal, political, religious, economic, and technological circumstances thus creating somewhat different urban structures. There have been particular phenomena characterizing a specific epoch or era and influencing urban developments in more than one culture region such as the colonial city of the 19th century and the socialist city of the

20th century both of which may, however, be subsumed under the superior concept of the culture regions.

In the present writer's opinion such cross-cultural studies have been somewhat neglected for a long time and should be promoted in the future since they are of greatest concern to urban geography in particular and to urban research in general.

REFERENCES

Bahr, J., Neuere Entwicklungstendenzen lateinamerikanischer Grosstadte (Recent tendencies of development of Latinamerican metropolises). *Geographische Rundschau*, 1976, pp 125-133.

Bahr J., Mertins, G., Idealschema der sozialraumlichen Differenzierung lateinamerikanischer Grostadte (Model of the social differentiation of Latinamerican metropolises). *Geographische Zeitschrift*, 1981, pp 1-33.

Beaujeu-Garnier, J.. Chabot, G., *Traite de Geographie Urbaine* (Urban geography), Paris, 1963.

Berry, B.J.L., *The Human Consequences of Urbanization*. London/ Basingstoke, 1973.

Berry, B.J.L. (ed.), Urbanization and counterurbanization. *Urban Affairs Annual Revies* vol. II. Beverly Hills, 1976.

Berry, B.J.L., Kasarda, J.D., *Contemporary Urban Ecology*, New York, 1977.

Borsdorf, A.S., Stadtische Strukturen und Entwicklungsprozesse in Lateinamerika (Urban structures and processes of development in Latin America). *Geographische Rundschau*, 1978, pp 309-313.

Boskoff, A., *The sociology of urban regions*, New York 2nd ed. 1970.

Burnley, I.H., Geographic-demographic perspective on the ecology of ethnic groups in Australian cities. In: Price, C.A., Martin, J.I. (ed.), *Australian Immigration. A Bibliography and Digest*. No. 3, part 1, 1975. Canberra, 1976, pp A124-A155.

Burnley, I.H., *The Australian Urban System. Growth, Change and Differentiation*, Melbourne, 1980.

Caralp, R., Les villes de la plaine du Gange (Cities of the Ganges Plain). *L'Information Geographique* vol. 36, 1972, pp 11-22.

Davies, R.J., The urban geography of South Africa. *Institute for Social Research*, Univ. of Natal, Durban, 1972.

Dawson, A.H., Warsaw: An example of city structure in free-market and planned socialist environments. *Tijdschr. Econ. Soc. Geogr.*, 1971, pp 104-113.

Dettmann, K., Damaskus. Eine orientalische Stadt zwischen Tradition und Moderne (Damaskus. An Islamic city between traditions and modernizations), *Erlanger Geographische Arbeiten* 26. Erlangen 1969

Fleure, H.J., Some types of cities in temperate Europe. *Geographical Review*, 1920, pp 357-374.

French, R.A., Hamilton, F.E.I. (ed.), *The Socialist City: Spatial Structure and Urban Policy*. Chichester/New York/Brisbane/Toronto 1979

Gormsen, E., Die Stadte im spanischen Amerika. Ein zeit-raumliches Entwicklungsmodell der letzten hundert Jahre (*The cities in Latin America. A Time-space Model of the Development of the Last Century*). Erdkunde, 1981, pp 290-303.

Griffin, E., Ford, L., A model of Latin American city structure. *Geographical Review*, 1980, pp 397-410.

Gutschow, N., *Die Japanische Burgstadt* (The Japanese castle to). Bochumer Geographische Arbeiten 24, Paderborn, 1974.

Hahn, F.G., Die Stadte der norddeutschen Tiefebene in ihrer Beziehung zur Bodengestaltung (The cities of the North German plain and their relation to the area's physiography). Stuttgart, 1885.

Hofmeister, B., *Stadtgeographie* (Urban geography). Braunschweig 1969, 4th rev. ed 1980.

Hofmeister, B., Die Stadtstruktur. Ihre Auspragung in den verschiedenen Kulturraumen der Erde (Urban structures. Their variations in the different culture regions). Darmstadt, 1980.

Hofmeister, B., Die Sudafrikanische Stadt. Versuch eines Strukturschemas der Stadte in der Republik Sudafrika (The South African city. A structural model of the cities in the Republic of South Africa). Die Erde 1982 (in print).

Holzner, L., World regions in urban geography. *Annals of the Assoc. of Amer. Geogr.*, 1967, pp 704-712.

Holzner, L., Sozialsegregation and Wohnviertelsbildung in amerikanischen Stadten, dargestellt am Beispiel Milwaukee (Social Segregation and the Development of residential areas in American Cities: The Case of Milwaukee). *Wurzburger Geographische Arbeiten* 37. Wurzburg, 1972, pp 153-182.

Holzner, L., Die kulutur-genetische Forschungsrichtung in der Stadtgeographie—Eine nicht-positivistische Auffassung (Culturalgenetic responses to processes of urbanization—an anti-positivist view). Die Erde, 1981, pp 173-184.

Huttenlocher, F., Stadtetypen und ihre Gesellschaften anhand sudwestdeutscher Beispiele (Urban types and their groupings: The case of Southwest Germany). *Geographische Zeitschrift*, 1963, pp 161-182.

Johnston, R.J., *City and Society: An Outline for Urban Geography*, Harmondsworth 1980.

Jones, R., *Essays on World Urbanization*. London, 1975.

Klimm, E., Schneider, K.G., Wiese, B., *Das sudliche Afrika* (Southern Africa). Darmstadt, 1980

Knubel, H., Modelle als Unterrichtshilfe fur die Stadtgeographie auf allen Stufen (Models as aids of teaching urban geography on various levels). In: *Beiheft zur Geographischen Rundschau* 1/1978, pp 40-48.

Koch, J., Tripoli (Libanon)—Eine orientalische Stadt im Wandel (Tripoli, Lebanon: A changing oriental city). In: *Beihefte, Atlas des Vordern Orients*, Series B no. 24. Wiesbaden, 1977, pp 107-129.

Kole, A., Die Geographie und die Kulturerdteile (Geography and the culture continents). In: *H.V. Wissmann-Festschrift*. Tubingen, 1962, pp 42-49.

Kolb, A., Geofaktoren, Landschafstgurtel und Wirtschaftserdtile (Geofactors, geographical zones, and economic continents). In: *Heidelberger Geographische Arbeiten* 15. Heidelberg, 1966, pp 29-36.

Lawless, R.I., Blake, G.H., *Tlemcen. Continuity and Change in an Algerian Islamic town*. London, 1976.

Leitner, W., Der Wandel per urbanen Raumorganisation der "Stadt am Goldenen Horn-Marmarmeer und Bosporus" (Changes of the urban spatial organization of the city at the Golden Horn, Marmara Sea and Bosporus). Arbeiten Inst. Geogr. Univ. Graz 24. Graz, 1981, pp 51-97.

Lichtenberger, E., The nature of European urbanism. *Geoforum* 4, 1970, pp 45-62.

Lichtenberger, E., Die europaische Stadt—Wesen, Modelle, Probleme (The European city—Nature, models, problems). Berichte zer Raumforschung und Raumplanung, 1972, pp 3-25.

Masai, Y., The contemporary Japanese townscape. *In*: *Assoc. of Japansse Geoger*. (ed.), *Japanese cities. A geographical approach*. Tokyo 1970, pp 97-108.

McGee, T.G., *The Southeast Asian city*. London, 1967.

Mellor, R.E.H., *Sowjetunion* (Soviet Union). Munchen 3rd ed. 1976.

Oberhummer, E., Amerikanische und europaische Stadte (American and European cities). In: *Memorial volume of the transcontinental excursion of 1912*. New York, 1915.

Passarge, S. (ed.), *Stadtlandschaften der Erde* (Urban landscapes of the world). Breslau., 1930.

Scargill, D.I., *The form of cities*, London, 1979.

Scholler, P., Stadt und Einzugsgebiet. Ein geographisches Forschungs problem und seine Bedeutung fur Landeskunde, Geschichte und Kultur raumforschung (The city and its hinterland. A problem in geographical research and its meaning for regional geography, history, and culture area research). Studium Generale, 1957, pp 602-612.

Seger. M., Strukturelemente der Stadt Teheran und das Modell der modernen orientalischen Stadt (Structural elements of the city of Teheran and model of the modern oriental city) Erdkunde, 1975, pp 21-38.

Smailes, A.E., The Indian city. A descriptive model., *Geographische Zeitschrift*, 1969, pp 177-190.

Tanabe, K., Intra-regional structure of Japanese cities. In: *Assoc. of Japanese Geogr.* (ed.), *Japanese Cities; A Geographical Approach.* Tokyo, 1970, pp 109-119.

Watson, J.W., *Social Geography of the United States.* London/New York, 1979.

FOUR

JURGEN FRIEDRICHS

PROGRESS IN COMPARATIVE URBAN RESEARCH

IN THIS paper the main problems of comparative research are sketched. Some solutions to these problems in the relevant literature are resumed, and finally the approach used in our former and the now ongoing research on "Urban Developments in Capitalistic and Socialistic Countries" is outlined.

Throughout the paper the focus is on comparative cross-cultural research. Several arguments have been presented in a former publication (Friedrichs 1978) and two recent papers (Friedrichs 1981, Kiehl et al. 1980).

PROBLEMS

Conducting comparative research implies a comparability of structures and processes. Thus, our working hypothesis has to be that we are able to identify regularities instead of assuming uniqueness of the elements under study. By "regularities" we may think of empirical regularities or even laws in the structure and the development of cities or agglomerations.

There are three types of problems—or even obstacles—faced by comparative cross-cultural research: (a) methodological, (b) theoretical, (c) data access and comparability.

(a) By methodological problems we refer to

Paper presented at the "European Meeting on Applied Urban Research", Essen, Oct. 2-4, 1981.

—the definition of indicators,
—equivalence of indicators,
—hypotheses required to link indicators to constructs, multilevel hypotheses, e.g. those relating economic changes in a country to economic changes in its capital city.

A case in point is the question of thresholds for the change or persistence of the structure of urban subareas. We have to define thresholds for each variable under scrutiny. This will lead to the problem of weighting the variables, since there may be a minor change in the variable value of variable X (e.g. criminality), but a major change in the value of variable y (e.g. divorce rate).

A second example is the structure of the explanations used. Studying changes in the urban structure immediately leads to the discussion whether the traditional Hempel-Oppenheim scheme of explanation holds true or instead "historical laws" or "historical explanations" should be introduced. (cf. Dray 1968, Hempel 1965:231, Stegmoller 1969-357). This problem has been stated by Stegmoller (ibid.) in the following form:

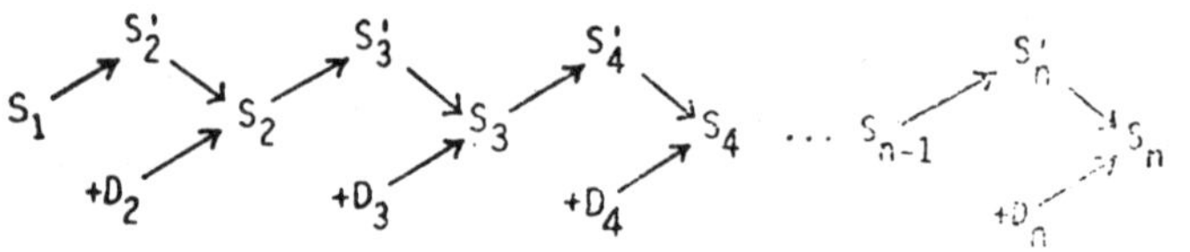

where $S_{1,2}$ statements describing events

$D_{1,2}$ specific singular facts

$S'_{2,3}$ events following causally from $S_{1,2}$

The problems rests in the search for laws explaining the multitude of descriptive statements and stating comparable initial conditions.

(b) The problems of *theory* can best be demonstrated by some examples from the literature. Evidently, there is no general theory explaining "urban structure" or "urban change". For methodological reasons this is impossible, since "structure" as well as "change" (or "development") do refer to sets of unspecified variables, each of them requiring particular theories. For example, the degree of segregation of a minority may be one of the variables in the set "structure". Thus, we do use many theories in urban research for different classes of phenomena: migration, land use, expansion, office location.

Comparative research has been conducted on indicators of the quality of living (e.g. Coates, Johnston & Knox 1977), selected ecological processes (e.g. Berry & Kasarda), urban density functions (e.g. Harrison & Kain 1974, Mills 1970), or in a more or less descriptive way, comparing different agglomerations (e.g. Burtenshaw, Bateman & Ashworth 1981, Dickinson 1967, French & Hamilton 1973, Hall 1979). The most widely used approach, which has lead to a large body of cumulative research is factorial ecology and social area analysis (e.g. Berry and Smith 1972). In Germany this approach has been adapted by Hamm (1981), using it now in his comparative international study (see the paper in this volume).

(c) The problems of *data access* are of a very pratical manner: How to get data on housing, migration, distribution of minorities etc. Definitions of variables differ among cities and countries, e.g. for "dwelling"; in addition, data accessible vary by level of agregation (block, census tract, district). Delineation of administrative units change over time, incorporation of fringe areas being the most prominent distorting fact.

Constructing equivalences of indicators seems the only strategy to cope with these problems. However, this requires theoretical sophistication and empirical studies, so we envisage again the problems listed under (a) and (b). Yet we all know that comparative cross-cultural research finally needs practical decisions, not always based on explicit theoretical reasoning. This is aggrevated by the fact that most comparative (urban) research is also longitudinal research, requiring data for several points in time.

THE PROJECT

Urban developments in capitalistic and socialistic countries

The project is directed toward a comparative analysis of the internal structure, the development and the planning in seven European capitals: London, Hamburg, Warzaw, Moscow, Paris, Vienna and Budapest. Capitals have been selected since we suppose urban development in a country can best be observed in their biggest city, which is in most cases as well the capital. (Hamburg is not the capital, but the biggest city in the F.R.G.).

This is the second phase of the project. The first phase has referred to London, Hamburg, Berlin (East), Warzaw and Moscow. The results have been published (Friedrichs 1978). This time we had to exclude Berlin (East) due to tremendous problems in getting recent data on the factual structure.

The study is designed to test different theories of urban development and the impact of different political, economic and social conditions on urban structure, change and planning. The area studied is the agglomeration.

Structure will change under specified conditions and this change may be viewed by the population or the administration as problematic. Arising social and economic (or fiscal) problems will require planning, which may eventually lead to further changes and new structures. The decay of the old housing stock close to the city centre may lead to programmes of urban renewal (or transformation into condominions) which in turn may lead to a gentrification, i.e. change in the structure of residents.

Some of the questions of the project are:

(i) Is there an ordered sequence of phases of urban change depending upon the effects of industrialization, changes in the employment structure, socio-economic differentiation of land uses and their locations ?

(ii) Do capital cities show a similar urban structure, e.g. the distribution of population by socio-economic and demographic variables, the distribution of land uses and housing stock ?

(iii) Are there at specific phases similar problems, leading to similar planning concepts, e.g. axes (development bands) or New Towns to steer sub-urbanization ?

(iv) Are there similar difficulties in urban planning, the implementation of programms and their success ? Can successful planning concepts be transferred from one (capital) city to another ?

Our theoretical approach is ecclectic. We start with an explicated version of the Burgess theory (Friedrichs 1977 : 101). In addition, we use hypotheses on land use, locational theories and propositions on societal differentiation. A preliminary causal model has been constructed. A further source for theory construction has been drawn from articles on stages on urban development (e.g. Abu-Lughod 1968, Duncan, Sabagh and Van Arsdol 1962, Dunn 1980, Sjoeberg 1960), refined by the results of our prior research. we just now work on a more precise definition of stages by specifying indicators and indicator-value combinations.

The access to data has been considerably improved compared to the prior study, enabling us to analyze processes on the census tract level. The data collection has, with the exception of Moscow, been completed. Results of the study will be available by the end of 1982.

REFERENCES

Abu-Lughod, J., The City is Dead—Long Live the City. Some Thoughts on Urbanity. In: S.F. Fava (ed.): *Urbanism in World Perspective*, New York, 1968.

Berry, B.J.L. and Kasarda, J.D., *Comparative Urban Ecology*. New York, London, 1977.

Berry, B.J.L. and Smith, K.B. (eds.), *City Classification Handbook*. New York, 1972.

Burtenshaw, D., Bateman, M. and Ashworth, G.J., *The City in West Europe*. Chichester, 1981.

Coates, B.E., Johnston, R.J. and Knox, P.L., *Geography and Inequality*. London, 1977.

Dickinson, R.E., *The City Region in Western Europe*. London, 1967.

Dray, W.H., "Explaining What" in History. In: M. Brodbeck (ed.), *Readings in the Philosophy of Social Science*. New York-London, 1968.

Duncan, B., Sabagh, G and Van Arsdol, M., Patterns of Urban Growth. *Am. J. Social* 67, 419-421, 1962.

Dunn, E.S., *The Development of the U.S. Urban System*, Vol. 1. Baltimore-London, 1980.

French, R.A. and Hamilton, F.E.I. (eds.), *The Socialist City*. Chichester, 1979.

Friedrichs, J., Stadtanalyse. Reinbek, 1977.

Friedrichs, J. (Hg.), Stadtentwicklungen in kapitalistishcen und sozialistischen Landern, Reinbek, 1978.

Friedrichs, J., Einige Probleme der vergleichenden Stadtforschung. Arbeitspapier fur die Sektion "Stadt—und Regionalsoziologie," Sitzung am 8.-10.4.1981 in Arnoldsheim, 1981.

Hall, P., *The World Cities* 2. rev. ed. London, 1977.

Hamm, B., Die Organisation der stadtischen Umwelt, Frauenfeld, 1977.

Hamm, B., Social Area Analysis and Factorial Ecology.. In: G.A. Theodorson (ed.), *Urban Networks*, Pennsylvania, 1981.

Harrison, D. and Kain, J.F., Cumulative Urban Growth and Urban Density Functions. *J. Urban Economy* 1, 1974, 61-98.

Hempel, C.G., Aspects of Scientific Explanation, New York-London, 1965.

Kiehl, K., Friedrichs, J., Droth, W. and Dangschat, J., Methodologische Probleme bei Vergleichen von Stadtentwicklungen. Referat zur Sitzung der Sektion "Stadt und Regionalsoziologie" am 9./10.5.1980 in Bad Homburg, 1980.

Mills, E., Urban Density Functions. Urban Studies 7, 1970, 5-20.

Sjoeberg, G. *The Pre-industrial City*, Glencoe, 1960, 111.

FIVE

ERLING BERGE

ON THE LIMITS OF SOCIAL ECOLOGICAL EXPLANATIONS IN COMPARATIVE RESEARCH

INTRODUCTION

IN COMPARATIVE research as elsewhere the important word is research. The "comparative" part just indicates one way of doing the research. It may be that the complexity of the world and the forever changing conjunctures of history put out of reach anything but incomplete and fragmented webs of understanding. But the goal is with us: to unravel and master the forces shaping us and our societies. We want to build a model of the world which will help mankind become master of its destiny.

One thread in this web is labeled social ecological theory. Every so often our separate small projects run across this one. Sometimes we even make it an anchor for directing our own threads of reasoning. But do we really know it? Do we know its strength or its weak parts?

The central problem of social ecological theory is to understand how a population organizes itself in adapting to a constantly changing yet restricting environment. The "ecological complex" (Duncan 1959) of population, organization, technology and environment are the main variables used in the studies of growth and development of social systems. A social ecological

Paper presented at the European Meeting on Applied Urban Research, 1981.

explanation in comparative research will thus be concerned with the variation in the interrelations among the variables of the ecological complex. Differences in development are then explained by differences in the interrelations of variables in the complex. What are the limits of such explanations?

Before we go into this problem a note on what is meant by "Limits" seem in order. Usually, limits may not be overstepped without suffering some kind of sanctions. The limits of scientific explanations are no exception to this. At best the theory will not support out statements, at worst we are talking nonsense. But from that it does not follow that we shall take care to stay within the limits posed by the present theory. Theories are there for us to work on so that our explanations stay within the limits of the theory and yet are explanations of the phenomena of interest.

Social ecological theory as it stands today (Hawley 1971, Berry & Kasarda 1977) encounters limits to its explanatory power at several points. But the way to treat these limits is not to resign from the effort to explain, but to rework the theory, to reinforce or replace its weak parts so that the present limits may be overcome, circumvented or moved further away.

If this is taken to be the aim, we still have the problem of identifying exactly what and where the limits of social ecological theory are. One well-tried way of finding such limits is to overstep them. Not having done much of that, I shall comment on some of the more established limits.

Limits due to data

Comparative research will today sooner or later—usually sooner—run into problems of obtaining comparable data. The standard way of treating this problem is to do something else, Some face the problem squarely and organize efforts to produce comparable data. A third way which should not be overlooked is to use theoretical models to bridge the gaps where data are missing. The study of factorial ecology will for instance point to the possibility of multiple ways of defining indexes of ecological structure (Hamm 1978) and maybe lists of equivalent indicators which in specific circumstances may substitute for each other.

Another possibility is to use models to compute a desired item, if information linked to it by theory is available. Demographic research may here provide examples (Keyfitz 1977).

Limits due to the choice of unit of analysis

The choice of unit of analysis must be done with regard to the problems one wants to investigate and according to the theory as it is established. What then is the appropriate unit for the study of urban development within social ecological theory?

To take for granted that it is the city, the urban area or the metropolitan region or some variation of this possibility is exactly what urban research usually has done. But what is "development", exactly what is this urban entity which "develops" and how does it "develop"? Is the city to be likened with a self-contained rational actor which develops in the same sense a human develops? Or is it more to be compared with the development of a natural ecological system? In other words, is the unit of analysis a non-actor systems* or an actor-system? Social ecological theoy does not indicate that this is a theoretical problem whose solution impose limits on the possible explanation. Exactly the same problem is encountered in cross-national research on development.

A central concept of the social ecological theory of development is "ecological expansion". Hawley (1950) and Duncan (1964) discuss societal evolution in a way indicating they think of industrial civilization as the unit which develops. But in Hawley (1979) the unit which develops is just referred to as a societal system. Shevky & Bell (1955) discuss development with reference to a concept of increasing scale of a society. For them, as for most of the students of development during the fifthies and sixthies, the natural unit for the study of development seemed to be the nation-state. But what kind of unit is a nation-state? A state is clearly an actor with certain responsibilities for a society. A nation is usually thought to be a

*A system is always composed of actors. An actor system is a system so organized that the system as a whole may be called an actor.

populaion with a common culture. It is clearly a non-actor system. Only rarely will one find coincidence of the boundaries of responsibility for a state and the boundaries of a culture.

The various processes generating what we call development, must in social systems have actors as executing agents. So what is it that generates the development of nation-state? Is it the activities of the individual actors of a culture or the activities of the system of state-actors? Posed this way the answer is obviously that they both affect the development of the nation-state. But until Wallerstein (1974; see also Wallerstein 1979, 1980; Chirot 1977 and Breiger 1981) published his investigation into the dynamic of the world system of states and large scale business enterprises, the implications for sociological theory of the marxist critique of mainstream theories of development seemed mostly unnoticed or ignored. Since then the problems of multilevel systems with different kinds of actors have cropped up everywhere. In order to contribute to the understanding of the development of different soical systems also social ecological theory must expand its scope to include multiple levels, different kinds of actors and systems, as well as specifications of how effects can be traced across levels, across system boundaries and how these effects are related to different types of actors. A beginning might be to recognize that social ecological theory as it stands today applies only to non-actor systems where there is no single actor or coalition of actors with any responsibility for the system as a whole (like states have responsibility for the society within their boundaries). This at least seems to be one possible interpretation of Hawley's (1979) speculations on the utility of an evolution model for the explanation of cumulative change.

In order to attack the problems connected with the duality of state and society (or nation) or at another level the duality of incorporated city and metropolitan region, the population and organization variables need to be refined by distinguishing among a population of human actors, a population of system responsible actors and a population of other incorporated actors (other than system responsible). The organization variable must differentiate between the organization of non-actor systems and the organization of actor systems. Both for non-actor systems and for actor systems of the various types of populations there will be levels of systems. Each hierarchy of levels can be summarized as follows:

Type of system organization	Non-actor systems of		
Type of population	System responsible actors	Organization actors	Human actors
Level			
Environment	World systems -of states -of cultures -of multinationals	Society	Society
Units of analysis	Society	Market	Social network
Agents of internal processes of the unit of analysis	All actors which are legitimate members of the society	All actors which are able to participate	Human actors

Type of system organization	Non-actor systems of		
Type of population	System responsible actors	Organization actors	Human actors
Level			
Environment	World systems -of states -of cultures -of multinational	World systems -of states -of cultures -of multinational	Society
Unit of analysis	State	Multi-national organizations	Organization
Agents of internal processes of the unit of analysis	Local system responsible actors and elected representatives from other populations	Member organizations	Human actors

If we from here return to the problem of doing comparative research on urban development, the problem must be restates as having to do with how technology and environment determine the parameters shaping the internal spatial distribution of the member actors of a society and their acivities. From an applied points of view the most interesting aspect lies in the possible degrees of freedom the system responsible actors of a society (the state, the cities and municipalities) have for influencing the internal spatial distribution of actors given the externally determined parameters. The appropriate unit for doing applied comparative urban research would then be societies where variations in externally determined parameters might be used as controls in the assessment of the efficiency of various efforts of system responsible actors to influence the characteristics of the urban regions within their societies.

REFERENCES

Berry, Brian J.L. and John D. Kasarda, *Contemporary Urban Ecology.* Macmillan, New York, 1977.

Breiger, Ronald, L., "Structures of Economic Interdependence Among Nations", in *Blau,* Peter M. and Robert K. Merton (eds.), *Continuities in Structural Inquiry.* Beverly Hills, Sage Publications, 1981

Chirot, Daniel, *Social Change in the Twentieth Century.* New York, Harcourt Brace Jovanovich, Inc. 1977

Duncan, Otis. D. "Human Ecology and Population Studies", in Philip M. Hauser and Otis D. Duncan (eds.), *The Study of Population,* pp 678-716. The University of Chicago, 1959.

Duncan, Otis D., "Social Organization and the Ecosystem," in *Faris.* Robert E.L. (ed.), *Handbook of Modern Sociology.* Chicago Rand McNally, 1964.

Hannan, M.T., *Aggregation and Disaggregation in Sociology.* Lexington, Mass., Heath, 1971

Hamm, Bernd, "Land Use and Segregation." Paper, U.psala, 9th World Congress of Sociology, 1978.

Hawley, Amos H., "Human Ecology". New York, Ronald Press, 1950.

Hawley, Amos H., *Urban Society: An Ecological Approach.* Ronald Press, New York, 1971.

Hawley, Amos, H. "Cumulative Change in Theory and in History", in Amos H., Hawley (ed.), *Societal Growth.* The Free Press, New York, 1979.

Keyfitz, Nathan, *Applied Mathematical Demography*, New York, Wiley, 1977.

Shevky, Eshref, and Wendel Bell, "Social Area Analysis: Theory, Illustrative Applications and Computational Procedures", Stanford: Stanford University Press, 1955.

Wallerstein, Inmanuel "The Modern World System: Capitalist Agriculture and the Origin of the European World Economy in the Sixteenth Century", New York, Academic Press, 1974.

Wallerstein Immanuel, "World Networks and the Politics of the World-Economy", in *Hawley*, Amos (ed.), *Societal Growth*, New York, Free Press, 1979.

Wallerstein, Immanuel, "The Modern World System II: Mercantilism and the Consolidation of the European World Economy 1600-1750". New York: Academic Press, 1980.

SIX

ALAN NORTON

POLICY ANALYSIS AS A STARTING POINT FOR COMPARATIVE STUDIES*

INTRODUCTORY

THIS paper is concerned with the conditions under which the international exchange of ideas on domestic policies can take place with the deepest possible understanding of their relevance and value in different national contexts. Policy ideas travel across national frontiers regularly and historical analysis shows that they have been remarkable influential. Leichter (1979) has recently shown that, in some policy areas at least, public policy-making has been "extraordinarily imitative". Policies are often adopted under the stimulus of knowledge of practice elsewhere, but with little understanding of the circumstances of their adoption and of consequent results and problems. The role of centres of higher learning in this process should be of first importance in that they are the places where resources for the study of society and its problems are concentrated and their field of reference is worldwide. In practice this is often not the case. Ideas spread with little benefit of learning. They spread with little understanding of the conditions to which they have been applied or evaluation of their consequeuces, and in some cases at least with little evaluation of their likely consequences in a new national environment. This, I suggest, is because they

*Paper presented at the European Meeting on Applied Urban Research, 1981.

tend to be adopted in a hurry to fulfil particular political needs and because the academic world has not generally succeeded in demonstrating its ability to provide a relevant contribution to policy-making under such conditions. It has not developed a methodology which is relevant and adequate to the task of making an appropriate contribution to the process of policy-making. I wish to elaborate this argument and to put forward a model which I hope will stimulate discussion on how centers of higher learning can best develop their capacity to assist policy-makers to gain the best understanding of foreign experience and its relevance to their problems.

Generally decision-makers do not reach across frontiers for ideas and experience. Rather, when confronted with a problem to which it is politically expedient to react, they grasp at an ill-digested concept derived from elsewhere, often without appreciation of its origins and its effects. Various attempts have been made to systematise the identification of promising forigen ideas and their adoption at local level, but I believe they have generally failed because of lack of appreciation of the methodology required. Study tours by officials and others, which are the commonest attempts to appreciate what can be learnt from foreign experience, can produce almost unbelievably superficial understanding of the phenomena observed. Simply the difficulty of understanding the differences between the functionaries called 'mayor' in different national systems can confuse understanding of conditions of feasibility and implementation.

It is elementary that each country has its own unique system and its own unique problems, arising from a unique history and culture. Social, economic, cultural, political and ideological systems have developed within the boundaries of nation states. These systems are inseparable from the development of each country's own language or languages. Dimensions that appear to cut across national frontiers—for example Marxist ideology—are in fact fragmented by the national systems, since the conditions that give them concrete meaning vary, sometimes radically. The concept of class itself, for example, is elusive in the light of the difference in class structure and so national class concepts from country to country.

The use of the term 'national system' needs some qualification. Nations are artefacts that can be created or split up over short historical periods, but each is characterised by a sharing of experience that is distinct and unique. That experience can be only very imperfectly understood even by a scholar who has given his life to appreciating it. Understanding across the boundaries of national systems is problematic. The need for linguistic translation presents further dilemmas in the transference of ideas and experience.

The use of an international language, which for historical reasons tends to be English or French, does not necessarily help, since the attachment of a common label in a foreign language to different phenomena can easily ensuare us into forgetting that we are not comparing like with like, as in the case of the word 'class' to which I have referred above. An illustration of likely confusion can be drawn from the area of work within which I locate this paper: I mean policy studies.

In all European languages of which I have any knowledge, excepting English, there is one word that connotes both policy and politics, from the root in the Greek *politike* to the Italian *politica*, the French *politique*, the German Politik and the Turkish *politika*. In English administration and politics the word *policy* is normally used a-politically for a course of action. *Politics* on the other hand usually means the pursuit of power or use of power in matters concerned with government, and particularly within and through the party system. In American usage it has the sense of manoeuvring or intriguing. These facts can result in considerable misunderstanding and confusion over the difference between a policy and a political issue if the semantic problems go unrecognised. Political scientists of course have their own definitions of policy and politics but, if a dialogue with policy-makers who do not share the scientific language is to be maintained, these cannot be shut off from national usages and kept in a kind of esoteric limbo.

Conceptual confusion if in my experience endemic in international conferences to an extent that severely limits their ability to agree meaningful resoultions and to share real understanding of what has been resolved. My experience has been mainly in international local government conferences. I have seen such a conference on regional problems founder on the pact that in no two countries is there a common understanding of what constitutes a region. Another conference on urban problems reached a high level of confusion and some acrimony in attempting to agree the resolution because of a failure to understand that, while the urban problem in Northern Europe, especially Britain, tends to be identified with the inner city, in the Mediterranean it tends to be identified with the outer city.

Experience motivating this paper

This paper is based on a range of subjective experience rather than upon structured research—experience that has led to conclusions about the practical approaches to research that can fulfil the needs which that experience has indicated. The experience may mostly be termed participant observation and has led to conclusions that have been reinforced by further experience. They relate to the policy seeking and adoption and could, I believe, be well substantiated empirically if sufficient research access to the policy-making process were possible. It is perhaps right that I should give more information about the range of experience concerned.

I have referred to attendance at international conferences in which the main participants have been local authority politicians and officials—some five of these in the last decade. For a number of reasons, some of which I have already indicated, organisers have not succeeded in achieving a common understanding among participants of the topic of discussion. Words such as environment, urban problems, region and decentralisation imply a sharing of concepts and realities which does not exist. They are not just 'fuzzy'—they are completely out of focus. The result, amongst some delegates at least, is a confirmation of their insular attitudes—a hardening of resistance to foreign ideas.

A second field of experience has been that of consultancies sponsored by international agencies—the World Bank, OECD, the World Health Organisation and the United Nations Development Programme—in which I have been reporting to mayors of metropolitan authorities—Nairobi and Istanbul—on institutional and policy matters. A consultancy is not defined as research: its success is normally judged by the acceptance of its recommendations rather than by the excellence of fact-finding and methodology. It is a case where the two English languge concepts of policy and politics converge and where Bismarck's dictum, "Die Politik ist die Lehre von Moglichen", applies in both senses: it is the science, or, as the usual English translation of the phrase has it, perhaps too inaccurately, the *art* of the possible. International agencies of course do their best to guarantee the quality of the consultants and their work, which they submit to expert assessment. Even in these cases there are reasons why, at its worst, the consultancy relationship can appropriately be compared to prostitution. It is for money, it is finite in time and carries no lasting obligations, it is confined to narrow terms of reference and implies no understanding between the parties beyond what is strictly necessary for mutual satisfaction. At its best, on the other hand, it can represent total commitment to the best available application of scientific knowledge, within the deepest possible understanding of a defined problem and its circumstances, in order to define measures that are both feasible in the short term and bring what are judged to be the most desirable welfare results in the long term. It requires an understanding of the relationship between the knowledge that is in the care of the scientific world as a whole and a complex of circumstances in a particular situation. It is a severe test of the application of scientific understanding. That so many consultancies fail to produce results, or the results intended, is a severe criticism of their deficiency, although it should be added that failure is frequently for reasons that cannot be blamed on the consultants. Often it is because of political changes which are unpredictable and in any event beyond the power of the consultants to control.

At best consultancy can be defined as a mutual learning process between consultant and client in which there is not only an exchange of knowledge and benefits but also an extension of understanding through an experimental process, since, given the high level of uncertainty that prevails about policy contingencies and the outcome of specific courses of action, any policy initiative must be regarded as experimental, and the shortfall between the intended and actual results deserves careful analysis. It can give access to knowledge and opportunities of pragmatic learning of a much greater richness than is normally available to academic research.

My argument assumes that the consultants can find common ground with the policy-makers and maintain their autonomy and objectivity. A base in institutions of higher learning can help to establish such conditions of autonomy, despite the sacrifice that conditions of confidentiality which are normally required by the client imposes. It enables the knowledge acquird to be fed, albeit in a restricted form, into the corpus of learning. The relationship, it may be noted, is quite different from that involved when the academic becomes an *employee* of the decision-makers. In that case the employers acquire rights related to the control of the employee's time and career, so that he cannot normally expect to maintain his independece.

A third type of experience explains the origins of my concern with cross-cultural influence in policy-making. It also introduces the dangers of colonialism in idea transfer. It derives from an early career as an administrator in West Africa during the immediate post-colonial period. I was alarmed by the facile application of policy ideas originating in Britain to a fundamentally different economic, social and cultural system and the unintended and unforeseen results. The colonial situation in which a policy vacuum is rapidly filled by foreign ideas because indigenous concepts relevant to newly defined issues appear absent or unacceptable is an extreme case, but one that is not fundamentally different from what can happen in developed countries when there is indifference about what measures are adopted in a policy area or where a foreign idea is attractive in terms of the narrow interest of one of the decision-makers or which the group of decision-makers represent e.g. the aggrandisement of the bureaucracy.

The last group of learning experiences is widely separate from the main African experience in time and character. Visits to Poland, Germany, Belgium and Italy in the last three years have shown the insularity of understanding of political and social phenomena within the British context. It has confirmed my belief that there is much of value to be learnt from comparison of systems if such comparison can be achieved in sufficient depth. This requires a sharing of knowledge of each other's systems—social, economic, political, cultural and semantic—to extent that demands heavy investment of scholars' time: something that at present rarely happens in the field of policy studies.

The comparative process

Comparison is fundamental to all mental understanding and is explicit or implicit in all research. From birth we realise our own physical identity by differentiation of concepts through a process of comparison, and the process gradually extends through the successive identification of family, class, cultural, civic, national and racial identity. We form a conceptual map of categories and of the relationships between categories, and we attach values to those categories and relationships. Such values tend to govern the direction of our thought and action. But our value-systems and their application to decision-making rest heavily on unreliable learning about reality, categories, relationships and probabilities. I suggest that it is the primary work of the social sciences to challenge this infrastructure of our value-systems and seek to reconstruct, by providing more satisfactory categories and a deeper and more comprehensive understanding of relationships and probabilities. Etzioni and Dubow (1970) argue that comparisons are liberating processes by means of which we "quickly discern that habits and beliefs that we consider fundamental may be viewed as marginal, and vice versa". As an instance they give treatment of drug addiction which, they state, tends to be treated in the United States by police, courts and jails, so that it is a shock to the American to find that in Britain it is regarded as a matter primarily for health authorities and doctors. Examples are legion.

Policy analysis: 'pure' and applied

Policy analysis may be 'pure' or applied. By 'pure' I mean that it may attempt to explain policy outcomes *post facto* from historical data. Alford (1969) provides an example: "Decisions, policy and government roles can be explained by a combination of situational, cultural and environmental factors." Such attempts may be found in very different styles. They may approximate to the historical tradition of explanation or they may use hard statistical data to analyse relationships on a probabilistic basis. Classification and comparison are basic to all such approaches, which are beset by many problems of logic and reliability. These problems arise partly from the uniqueness and limits of predictability of social events; the non-falsifiability of hypotheses in the social sciences and their lowness in information content in terms of the non-tautological propositions that can be derived from them (Popper, 1959); and the difficulty of identifying invariant units of value that are truly equivalent or comparable, or even satisfactory indicators of what it is aimed to measure (Verba, 1977).

On the other hand, policy analysis may be in the 'applied' mode. It may seek to solve social problems in order to fulfil political purposes. These are normally overtly ethical purposes: to reduce the quantum of suffering or injustice or to increase human welfare, for example. The purposes may of course be amoral or egoistic. That texts on policy analysis assert the welfare aims of its practice or emphasise the need to extrapolate the value judgments that are made in the process is most important for ethical standards and understanding. An extreme example of the problem-solving approach is Aaron Wildavsky's *The Art and Craft of Policy Analysis* (1979). To him it is essentially the attempt to solve potentially soluble problems. The lesser constituent is 'intellectual cogitation', which includes comprehending, institutional planning and rational choice of alternatives: the greater constituent is 'social interaction' which of course includes political interaction—involvement in a process of understanding and testing with participants in decision-making and implementation. If I understand his definition rightly, policy analysis involves an action-learning situation. The analyst must plunge into the institutional world of markets and politics, risk making partial and imperfect calculations, learn from the inter-action of minds in policy-making situations and the exchange and bargaining of decision-making, seeking to correct rather than to avoid error, to agree conclusions rather than to impose them and to stimulate re-action rather than to inspire obeisance. Textbooks emanating from American schools of policy analysis tend to put a higher emphasis on rational decision-making techniques. Thus MacRae (1975) defines it as embracing reasoned valuative discourse, definition of problems, proposals of alternatives, the application of models, methods for testing models and a care for intermediate goals and feasibility.

However defined, applied policy analysis is meant to act at the point where scientific understanding contributes to governmental policy. If we accept the aim of influencing policy or of the authoritative attribution of values, the point of involvement is where governmental decision formation is accessible to scientific learning. This may be very close to the point at which decisions are taken: direct advice to a minister or to an executive mayor. Or it may be less close but within the governmental machinery; or it may be outside the governmental machinery, in the political opposition or a pressure group. It may be long-shot: indirectly through the academic community or influence on public opinion. But the further we are away from inter-action with the decision-making elite, the less the opportunity for action learning in social interaction and therefore the less informed the analysis is likely to be about the nature of the contingencies involved. It may be added, if you believe that power corrupts, that the less likely the work is to be corrupted by proximity to power.

What I have termed 'pure' policy analysis can contribute to applied analysis in a number of ways. It develops frameworks of analysis. These may attempt comprehensiveness. Leichter (1979) for example builds on the proposition by Alford quoted above a listing of decision factors in four groups: situational, structural, cultural and environmental, which he attempts to use to explain expenditure priorities in different countries. Analysis of aggregate comparative statistics on a global scale can throw light on few of the factors involved. To handle a reasonably wide range of factors, Leichter takes a specific field of policy and limits the analysis to four countries.

Studies with a much sharper focus and stricter controls may be more helpful. Hofstede's *Culture's Consequences* (1980) for example gives valuable insights into the character of motivation in different cultures. The concepts and indices which he uses—of power distance between superior and subordinate, of uncertainty avoidance, of individuality and masculinity—although based on data collected in an international corporation, surely have a high relevance to the character of public decision-making. Hofstede's short reviews of the history of ethno-centrism—the tendency to be dominated by the characteristics and assumptions of one's own national or racial culture—and of overcoming the monodisciplinary approach—are valuable and I wish I had space to expand on them. He comments, ' The primitive ethno-centrism of many cross-cultural studies of organisational behaviour has been, I believe, one of the main reasons for the lack of advance of the art.'' The same may perhaps be suggested with regard to comparative policy analysis. 'Pure' analysis can contribute to breaking down the ethno-centrism and disciplinary limitations of our thinking, providing not only conceptual structures but suggestive *a priori* theory, methodological ideas and historical and geographical perspective. They can help us to enrich our ideas about behaviour and about the relationships between economic, social and cultural factors, enriching the tentative explanations we can put forward in a concrete situation of applied policy analysis. But this 'top-down' thinking has to be met by 'bottom-upward' thinking and understanding. There is no alternative to plunging into the complexities of the particular policy situation under study and gaining not only an appreciation of the relevant hard data and the economic, social and cultural environment with all the constraints it imposes, but also of the pattern of social relations among the decision-makers and those on whom they depend. Most important are the values and motivation, not only of the decision-makers but also of the implementors.

One very briefly described example from Africa, not from the myriad cases of misapplication of European ideas on that continent but of the transfer of policy ideas from one capital city to another. In city A, a house self-build scheme has worked quite well and a policy to transfer the ideas from city A to city B was sponsored by an international agency. But the economic system, land tenure, population pressure, socio-economic class structure, cultural values, political system and other basic factors were quite different: the approach was quite inadequate in relation to the scale of the problem and failed to take up and utilise the considerable potential indigenous resources available. The lack of enthusiasm for the policy shown by the local people reflected their wisdom but the development of adequate alternatives required a study in which an understanding of economic, social, cultural and political factors was essential. It was necessary to build up a mental model of how these factors interacted, based not only on available data and their analysis but also on exploration of the knowledge and attitudes and ideas of a large number of those involved in the decision-making and implementational processes, and to keep testing conclusions and ideas against their knowledge. The most difficult institutional problems related to the restructuring necessary for policy initiatives on which it was possible to reach agreement, and the related problem of securing the appointments of competent implementors. Some of the hopes of gain by prominent officials inevitably have to be disappointed while others will be fulfilled. This is perhaps the most delicate ground of all. The package of ideas with which the analytical process started was broken up, some ideas introduced from elsewhere and the comparative dimension that was so important at the early stage of analysis slowly receded from the mind as a convincing interpretation of the local situation took shape. When a policy process is set in train, the practical learning process should of course be rapid and may be expected to pose an indefinite series of new policy problems. In some cases the comparative process may again be important in the search for radical solutions.

The place of comparative studies in policy analysis

I shall now attempt to generalise about the role of comparative studies in applied policy analysis and then to define a practical approach which I hope will be of value in establishing the international links which I believe to be fundamental if our studies are to escape from ethno-centrism.

In a recent paper (pending) J.D. Stewart has distinguished between three domains in policy development: Policy derivation, policy adoption and policy justification. Comparative studies can play an important role in policy derivation as part of the process of idea exploration and the discovery of possibilities. Questions such as "How has the problem been defined?", "What objectives have been set?", "How have resource needs been met?", "What has been the definition of the roles or jobs involved?," What level of decentralisation for policy-making, resources-raising and implementation is possible and desirable?"—any of these and many others may derive illumination from the comparative context. Probing into deeper issues may challenge our ordering of values and ensure that it is not based merely on unreasoning acceptance. To ask in a comparative context "What objectives have priority?", "In what assumptions are extant policies embedded?", "What are the implications of the methods of motivation of implementors and the public?", "What is the mix of economic and social benefits and disbenefits involved for the groups affected?" may help us to understand the outcomes of different policy proposals in new ways. They have also implications for policy justification, since this, relying to a large extent on the rational model of decision-making, requires the study of alternatives. In fact, examination of a policy area in another country may well be structured by the phases of policy derivation (its origins in the definition of the problem concerned and the constraints on its form and development), adoption (exploration of its political rationale) and justification. In such a study the examination takes a historical form, aiming at the analysis of experience. Each phase should benefit from being seen in relation to the whole: something not possible except speculatively in ongoing policy analysis.

The methodology of learning from experience elsewhere is a field that has to a large extent been neglected in academic studies. It requires its own methodology, to some extent distinct from the normal academic pursuits of categorisation, theory construction and testing of propositions. It is far from orthodox scientific method: it can proceed by suggesting and destroying analogies—scattering ideas somewhat wildly prior to rigorous testing of their relevance to wildly varying situations. It can break down ethno-centrism by challenging our view of reality, but also enable us to appreciate more clearly the ethnic and other local peculiarities which require understanding if policy choice is to be relevant to locally defined problems.

Definition of an approach to comparative studies for policy analysis

Problem selection

Leichter (1979) has shown not only how public policy-making can be extra-ordinarily imitative: he has also shown how it is extraordinarily reactive. Major innovations tend to be reactions to perceived critical conditions. When these reactions take place they are often imitative of reactions elsewhere. They are influenced by a superficial understanding of one or two foreign systems. Comparative policy studies need to identify critical areas before a crisis or catastrophe forces structural change in policy, so that understanding exists in depth of the experience of relevant policies in other countries which can enrich the response when it is necessary.

The broad study of the main aspects of the environment of foreign policies and policy-making is important not only for the interpretation and explanation of a particular policy focus but also for the identification of issues in foreign countries which have been ignored locally—those issues which have been consciously or unconsciously omitted from public debate—non-decisions and non-perceptions. This is a process of sensitisation to considerations and possibilities.

In terms of studies relating to the second country, this phase is perhaps best described as system appreciation—the observation of the actual and its comparison with our norms. Vickers' description of this process in another context is relevant (Vickers, 1965, 1968).

Because of the complexity of the task and problems over language and over limitations on the time and resources available, direct dependence on scholars in other countries is inevitable.

The ideal is a research partnership between experts in two different countries, each alerting the other to key sources and correcting each other's misperceptions. Without such pairing it is difficult to see how the necessary level of system appreciation can be built up cross-nationally, and how the simultaneous appreciation of lacunae in domestic policy and relevance of foreign experience can be achieved. Attempts to develop this approach with respect to three, four or more countries would rapidly compound the problems of complexity and lead to a geometrical progression in the degree of superficiality. World congresses on domestic policy issues lead to the maximum possible superficiality, if not maximum possible misunderstanding, if their agenda is concurrent learning about systems in all the countries involved.

Policy description

The form of partnership described is also fundamental to the description of policies within a defined area of interest. Study of objectives, formal and informal statements of objectives, organisation for implementation, prescriptive rules, purposive behaviour within such rules, outputs and their control, the explanation of the gap between intention and achievement and many other aspects of policy require description if they are to be used for policy comparison. A description is of course always a simplification of reality or a model of what is understood to happen: it is inevitably an abstraction from limited observation supported by such objective data as are available. It is a 'unique model', particular to a time and place and does not itself require any 'invariable unit of comparison' of a kind that has been prescribed as a necessary element in theory construction through the comparative method. The model is an hypothetical one that can be tested against expert judgment in a partnership arrangement and revised until it is consistent with observation by any number of experts.

The policy model or description requires explanation in terms of its context—of the economic, social, cultural and other values, resources and constraints that have determined it. This explanation is a 'bridging' model, explaining the relationship between it and the model of the environment.

The descriptive phase can also cover self-criticism—the evaluation of the policy approach by participants and observers 'within the culture'. The description may usefully be framed in the form of answers to a series of key questions which are of a sufficiently general nature to be answered in a similar way for both first and second countries. Thus the material will be structured to facilitate comparisons. Where there is no satisfactory answer to a question, that fact will indicate the incompleteness of the model.

Policy comparison as a means of policy derivation

Part of a rationale for policy comparison as an aspect of policy derivation has been given in earlier part of this article. A key question in comparing each part of the models must be "What new approaches can be derived from achievements and experience in country A for policy derivation and policy change in country B?"

The transfer of an aspect of policy from one country to another must be tested by a rigorous analysis of feasibility and expected consequences in the quite different environment. It involves a process of reality judgment following a perception that a particular observation may have relevance to a domestic problem. The foreign idea is only the beginning of a difficult process of relating, developing and testing a new possibility for action, following many assessments of local realities. It may lead to an empirical process of testing, evaluation in practice and adoption. But at this point any relationship to the comparative act which began the train of policy development is likely to be remote if not forgotten.

CONCLUSION

Comparative policy studies have a role to fulfil in securing that the transference of policy ideas happens with full understanding of sources and full exploration of implications, as well as that it happens at all. They deserve rapid development as a major aid in enabling governments—both central and local—to identify more appropriate means of response to the problems that beset them. Partnership between higher education and research institutions, and between their members, in different countries provide an excellent and probably irreplaceable means to promote them.

What conditions should we require of such partnership? Partners should share interest in similar policy areas and have as thorough an understanding as they can achieve of the policy areas concerned in their own countries. They should also be committed to studying the same fields of policy and the complex environment that determines action in those fields in their partner's country, discussing with him sources of knowledge, concepts and interpretations. Obviously, understanding is difficult without mutual knowledge of languages and it is desirable that there is a serious investment of time in learning about each other's semantics as well as about each other's systems. Each partner's interpretation of policy in the other country would be criticised by his partner there. Each partnership would have means of recognition within the academic and research communities in the two countries—particularly where these are concerned with policy analysis. Perhaps the scope of understanding could be expanded by linking partnerships based on different disciplines: for example a pairing of political scientist with a pairing of economists. Policy analysis is essentially multi-disciplinary and enrichment of cross-disciplinary understanding is important in the context of cross-cultural understanding.

Each partner might seek involvement in the policy definition process in his own country, both to deepen his understanding of that process and to contribute ideas and analysis, some of which will have sprung from his work on policy comparison in his partnership. He would in particular have a role in ensuring that ideas and experiences of the other country are taken into account with as deep as possible understanding of their nature and conditions.

REFERENCES

Alford, Robert, *Bureaucracy and Participation: Political Culture in Four Wisconsin Cities*, Rand McNally, Chicago 2, 1969.

Etzioni, Amitai, and Ferderic L., Dubow, *Comparative Perspectives: Theories and Methods*. Little Brown & Co., Boston. Introduction, 1970.

Hofstede, Geert, *Culture's Consequences*. Sage, Beverly Hills and London, 1980.

Leichter, Howard M., *A Comparative Approach to Policy Analysis*. Cambridge University Press, Cambridge 65, 1979.

MacRae, Duncan Jr.. "Policy Analysis as an Applied Social Science Discipline" in *Administration and Society*, vol. 6 No. 4, 363-88, 1975.

Popper, Karl R., *The Logic of Scientific Discovery*: Hutchinson, London, 1959.

Stewart, J.D., "Guidelines to Policy Derivation" in *Approaches in Public Policy-Making* (Steven Leach, ed.). Allen & Unwin, London.

Verba, Sidney, "The Cross-National Programme in Political and Social Change: a History and Some Comments" in *Cross-National and Comparative Survey Research Theory and Practice* (E. Szalai and R. Petrella, ed.). Pergamon, London, 1977. 188-92.

Vickers, Geoffrey, 1965. *The Art of Judgment*. Chapman & Hall, London and Basic Books, New York. (1968). *Value Systems and Social Process*. Tavistock, London and (1970) Penguin Books, Harmondsworth.

Wildavsky, Aaron, *The Art and Craft of Policy Analysis*. Macmillan, London and Basingstoke, 1979.

SEVEN

KLAUS R. KUNZMANN

STRUCTURAL CHANGE IN OLD INDUSTRIAL AGGLOMERATIONS
First Experiences from A Comparative Research Project*

INTRODUCTION

SINCE the late sixties the process of structural economic change has considerably proceeded in those European countries with an industrial tradition reaching back to the late 18th and early 19th century. The major characteristics of this change are widely recognized, including changes in industrial concentration, ownership patterns and geographical location and distribution of industrial enterprises. These changes occurred in the context of technological innovations, rationalization processes and changing social and cultural attitudes and aspirations, factors which are mutually interdependant. The effects of structural economic change have been felt most severely and generally in old industrial areas of Northwest Europe, which are orginally based on the exploitation of coal, on textile mills, on the production of iron and steel and on iron and steel derived products. This is true as well for those regions which have handled the products to colonial markets in exchange to raw materials and minerals, timber and agricultural products.

The industrial region around Liverpool in Britain and the Ruhrgebiet, the once powerful coal and iron based polycentric agglomeration in the heart of the Federal Republic of Germany

*Paper presented at the European Meeting on Applied Urban Research, 1981.

are two of these old powerful and affluent industrial regions. Today the populations of both regions suffer from the social, economic and environmental consequences of this structural economic change.

These two regions are the geographical study areas of this research project, which has brought together researchers of two urban and regional planning departments at Liverpool Polytechnic and the University of Dortmund. Their research objective is to identify, to analyse and to compare 'Community and Public Authority Responses to Changing Economic Structure in Old Industrial Areas' using both regions as a reference area for empirical investigations. Theoretical, methodological and organizational experiences from a pilot study and ongoing main research project are reported thereafter.

The nature and some problems of international comparative research

International comparative research in the field of urban and regional studies has only a very young tradition. Apart from compiling basic data and information on urban and regional planning and on related issues, mainly done by international institutions as the ECE, the OECD or the EEC, very few international comparative studies in the proper sense have been carried out hitherto.

Only recently a few pilot projects comparing planning policies in Britain, with those of the Netherlands or Germany are recorded.

There are many reasons for this obvious lack, but most of them arise from the immense theoretical, methodological, organizational and last but not least financial and political problems related to international comparative research.

Purposes of research

The experience made so far in the context of the RUHR-MERSEY-project and its preceding Pilot Project seem to be so essential for future comparative research that we feel it important to describe them frankly in some detail. In preparing this ongoing project it soon became obvious that in designing an international comparative research project early and urgent attention should be given to questions concerning the purpose of such research.

Moreover, it turned out to be wise that in large and complex projects it may be the case that a (limited) number of specific purposes is to be selected rather than one all-embracing purpose.

Consequently it was important to discuss at an early stage how far aspects of the project were intended:

(i) to identify common structures in each region?
(ii) to identify marked differences between them?
(iii) to seek empirically based generalization?
(iv) to establish new data or analysis for policy-makers?

In order to clarify the purposes of research it was necessary to try and locate the proposed work within some familiar social science frameworks. We asked for example how far aspects of the project were intended:

(i) to generate common hypotheses?
(ii) to test hypotheses and to develop theories?
(iii) to explain specific phenomena?
(iv) to describe certain events or processes?
(v) to isolate certain policy variables?

These questions related as well to the academic dispute between 'disciplinary research' as against to 'policy research' in urban and regional planning studies.

Methodological questions

The difficulties of methodology most often mentioned in discussions of international comparative research fall into two groups. First there are those which may be found in *any* (comparative) social science work and are *not* exclusive to international projects as:

—research organization and management (e.g. logistics);
—matching of data with theoretical formulations;

—research skills;
—choice of appropriate methods.

However, these problems are likely to be encountered in more acute forms when they occur in an international project. From our Pilot Project experiences we draw some general conclusions for future international comparative studies.

In addition of these, there are two major methodological problems which are held to be specifically associated with international comparative work, as:

—matching of data, definitions and categories between countries, and
—difficulties of language and communication at all levels.

Matching of data with theoretical formulations

This is one of the 'classic' problems of all social science research. First of all there are problems of availability of data, e.g. the degree to which data are published or unpublished, accessible to researchers, qualified by conditions of confidentiality etc. Secondly there are serious difficulties of ensuring that the data do in fact correspond to the theoretical categories implied by one's approach.

It follows that the great care must be exercised to see that *either* the theoretical perspective adopted does fit the data that are available *or* that fresh data can be collected (or collecting data manipulated) to ensure a reasonable fit. A pilot project will allow time for the study of this kind of problem.

Choice of appropriate methods

In many ways this issue lies at the heart of the academic success of much social science work. The pitfalls are fairly obvious. No amount of numbering-crunching is liable to lead to a breakthrough in knowledge if the aim of the project is to develop hypotheses rather than to test existing theory. But such data collection will be indispensable if the objective is to lay bare (say) the changing economic fortunes of a region in some detail. A scrupulous review of the literature on the role of the state in twentieth century capitalist countries is not likely to be very useful if the project was supposed to be focussed on an international comparison of the success of specific regional policies in two regions.

Case studies are a very popular method on a lot of social science research but can remain at the level of good academic journalism unless they are used to illuminate, test or develop certain specific hypotheses. Case studies are virtually indispensable in penetrating into the detailed operations of (say) local authorities, individual firms or trade unions which a more generalised study of aggregate information would fail to reveal.

Matching of data and definitions between countries

This is the first of the two very specific problems associated with international comparative social science research and again it is a classic problem of the field, so much so that attention is so focussed on it as to obscure certain other important issues. The problems are well-known. First the levels or depth of data may be very different, highly detailed and disaggregated in one country, highly generalised in the other. Or, equally detailed data may exist in each case but much more accessible in one country rather than the other (e.g. on grounds of confidentiality).

Most commonly, we encounter difficulties of taxonomy and definition (language!). Industrial and occupational definitions are a familiar example. A train driver and a University professor are 'civil servants' (Beamte) in Germany but not in Britain. 'Derelict Land' evokes a bundle of specific associations in the brain of a British planner which are incompatible with the respective associations a German planner will have. Britain's Standard Industrial Classification (S.I.C.) and its census definitions of 'household' have changed over time rendering detailed historical analysis problematical. Definitions of 'unemployment' and 'poverty' are fraught with different kinds of problems of interpretation (and bureaucratic creditibility).

The standard way out of these difficulties superficially appears easy. First and foremost, a very careful study of the problem in detail with a high degree of interpretation and commentary being provided between the members of the national teams in the context of a pilot project before any major investigations is indispensable. In addition, wherever possible and appropriate—mainly for comparative national data—use can be made of data series prepared by international agencies (such as UN, OECD, EEC) which ensure that a high degree of compatability is present. Both ways, however, do not solve all difficulties of crosscultural comparisons.

Research organisation and management appears to be a function of the number of research workers, the number of different disciplines and a negative linear function of their administrative abilities.

The actual pattern of collaborative work should be clarified to the greatest extent possible. For example how far are (two) international groups to work on themes (e.g. the economy) separately with rather widely-spaced comparisons *via* working papers on the one hand, or on the other, should they try to work in a more truly international way on each theme with much more frequent 'low level' contacts? How far should workers in country A actually carry out work in country B and *vice versa*?

The problems of *research skills and language* seem a trivial issue. Nevertheless problems may arise for several reasons. For example the project may be inadequately specified, too vague and imprecise and the researches may become unwilling, overburdened once they accepted to co-operate and the necessary degree of precision has been reached.

The study regions and their major problems

On a first sight both the Ruhrgebiet and Merseyside have very little in common. Their differing size and the enormous difference in its population figures and working force alone seem to be unequal preconditions for any kind of scientific comparison. In addition there are other features which characterize more differences than similarities of the two regions. Whereas the Ruhrgebiet is based on coal and iron, Merseyside's former wealth derives from the function of Liverpool as a major port with its related industry and commerce. Even the spatial structure of the two regions rather represent two differing spatial systems. The Ruhrgebiet is a polycentric agglomeration comprising a few independent cities, functioning as important urban centres and a number of smaller, even semi-rural communities. Merseyside in turn is a region dominated by one big urban centre, Liverpool, which is surrounded by a number of small industrial communities.

In these terms the Ruhrgebiet is more comparable with the whole North-West Region of Britain. The North West has a population of around six million people, a multi-facetted industrial base including coal and steel production, two major cities (Manchester and Liverpool), a large number of smaller cities and towns and sophisticated inter and intra-urban transportation systems.

Other indicators, however, describing the social and economic structures show remarkable similarities of the Ruhrgebiet and Merseyside. Both regions are currently characterised by:

—a process of economic decline which was originally caused by the weakness of the dominant regional economic production complex: the strong interlinked coal-steel-chemicals complex with its affiliated mechanical engineering sector in the Ruhrgebiet, and the port with its associated service sector and the port-orientated ship-yards, engineering and food industry in Merseyside;

—an above-average high and protracted unemployment situation particularly affecting the young as well as older and unskilled workers;

—the outmigration of young, mobile and well-trained workers to other regions in Southern Germany/England with the resulting change in population structure and overall population decrease;

—migration of firms and households from the traditional innercity living and working areas into the edges of the conurbation, triggered by economic displacement processes, land-use and housing policies;

—the loss of the traditional functional mix of residential and industrial areas for dock, mine and steel workers which in addition has been aggravated by major clearance schemes

(for example in Liverpool) or by inadequate land and housing policies in both regions; and by
—large stretches of unused or partly used land of old mining and industrial areas which hamper balanced development.

Any comparison between regions in two different countries must take account of their integration into the national development and policy scene. The considerable economic problems on Merseyside can only be comprehended with knowledge of the current British economic policy. And a comparison of unemployment rates has to be seen, for example, against the very different national policies regarding the immigration of foreign workers.

The Pilot Project clearly showed that a comparison of regions in different countries cannot be confined solely to a description and statistical survey of sectoral and spatial structural change. It is more important to understand these changes as a *political process* and to ask how the pressing problems are or should be solved. The necessary structural changes can only be successfully achieved if the negative consequences and burdens on the population concerned can be diminished or even avoided from the outset. It is therefore vital not just to monitor the consequences of structural economic change but also to record the *reactions* of the population either as workers in the companies or as inhabitants of old and new housing areas. Their needs are essentially the framework conditions for the measures implemented by business and the various state and community administrations and which in turn are reactions to problems posed externally. By this they themselves become factors in political decision-making processes. The varying reactions of national institutions and social groupings must be observed and analysed for their mutual and reciprocal dependence on the direction, speed and form of structural economic change to assist in forecasting possible and probable development trends in structural change and formulating counter-measures at the right time.

A comparison of developments in regions of Great Britain and Western Germany is well suited to such an attempt, since the causes of economic change are basically identical, while national differences in terms of timescale, interrelationships of social groups, political institutions and traditions, interplay of economic and political 'philosophies' and hence the forms of reaction overall would seem to be sufficiently marked to enable a comparative analysis to reveal their influence on structural change.

The comparison of actions and reactions, measures and objectives as well as plans and programmes can, on the basis of case studies on Merseyside and in the Ruhrgebiet give the participating groups and public decision-makers in both regions some ideas for coping with the consequences of structural economic change.

Structural change in older industrial regions

The most significant finding of the Pilot Project was that the Ruhrgebiet and Merseyside showed remarkable similarities in terms of structural change. This was manifested in two distinct but related ways: the declining economic base and the changing spatial structure of both regions.

The declining economic base

Changes in international demand, the rise of multinational enterprises in all economic sectors coupled with changing technologies (generally towards more capital-intensive modes of production) have been eroding the economic base of both the Ruhrgebiet and Merseyside. In the Ruhrgebiet the decline of coal and more recently of steel have produced huge job losses in both these sectors whilst on Merseyside the declines have led to an inexorable reduction in the role of the port of Liverpool. In both regions these declines in the key industries have led to losses in related industries and now even those growth industries brought in largely as a result of state intervention during the 1960s, e.g. the car industry, have themselves begun to decline. Although the quaternary sector (government employment, banking, insurance, finance, professional and scientific work) has been growing in both regions, such growth has been slower than in other regions (e.g. South

East England, Munich, Frankfurt) and the proportion of this sector is lower than in other regions. The net result has been that growth in neither 'imported' nor the indigenous quaternary sectors has been sufficient to offset the massive losses experienced in the traditional economic bases so that both regions have experienced sustained and considerable losses of jobs.

These falling levels of jobs coupled with a workforce which was expanding (due to age structure in both regions) has led to very considerable unemployment, increasingly among younger people. During the 1960s the West German economy was sufficiently buoyant for the Ruhrgebiet to absorb—in connection with social policy measures—the job losses in the coal and iron sector. Unemployment figures fell again and the area seemed to recover quickly from the first major post-war recession of 1966/68. But since the 1970s large-scale unemployment has emerged. The percentage increases have in fact been comparble to those of Merseyside, but Merseyside, having failed to recover in 1966/68 began in a worse situation.

Both regions have a greater proportion of long-term and youth unemployment than their national averages; both have unemployed people with either no skills or skills which are in low demand for existing or newer forms of development; both areas have (small) growth sectors which are not providing jobs suitable for the unemployed and relevant workers; in both Merseyside and the Ruhrgebiet what little growth does exist is not providing longer-term prospects for young people. In both regions levels of educational attainment are well below the national averages; both perform badly when compared with their respective national averages in terms of overall growth in employment and other economic indicators (e.g. real disposable incomes, capital employed per worker, etc.)

In both regions too, the geographical locations of the older declining productive capacity and the newer expanding plants have led to changes in the spatial structure which are also remarkably similar and which form the second major feature of the Pilot Project's findings.

The changing spatial structures of the Ruhrgebiet and Merseyside

The major problem of spatial change found in both regions is one of decentralisation from the older urbanised 'cores' to the suburbs and outer fringes. We must, however, distinguish carefully the nature or causes of decentralisation between the case of employment (or productive capacity) on the one hand and residential activities on the other.

Decentralisation of jobs is very little due to actual physical migration of premises and plants and is almost wholly accounted for by the differential patterns of 'births' or expansion and 'deaths' or declines *in situ.* Thus, decline in the inner parts of the urban fabric is almost always due to the complete closures of individual plants and reductions in their labour force by redundancies and/or technological change. For historical reasons, the older and less efficient industries and plants tend to be located on the inner parts of the Ruhrgebiet (e.g. inner Dortmund, Duisburg, Herne) and Merseyside (e.g. the old docks, shipyards and other riverside, port-related industries).

By contrast, the newer more efficient and profitable industries tend to be located in (or have been introduced into) the suburbs and outer fringes of the metropolitan regions (e.g. Unna, Kamen Kirkby, Ellesmere Prt, Halewood). In both regions, this preference (by capital) for outer locations seems to have been dictated by the need for more extensive (e.g. production line) processing on cheaper land with good uncongested road access to the motorway and autobahn systems being important factors.

However, if the changing spatial structure of employment is almost wholly accounted for by the differential patterns of industrial 'births' or 'deaths' rather than by migration, the reverse is true of population decentralisation. In this case, both regions have witnessed the actual physical migration of people from inner to outer areas. It is certainly true that a small proportion of the total change is accounted for by people leaving the regions altogether (mostly working class people from the inner areas seek work in more prosperous parts of Britain and Germany) or entering the regions from elsewhere (mostly middle class people pursuing a migratory status ladder) to seek housing in the more salubrious suburbs.

But the great bulk of moves (as research elsewhere has shown) have been made within the regions themselves. Certainly in the British case this can be clearly distinguished into two types of relocation: first non-voluntary whereby inner city houses are cleared (with or without redevelopment and then usually at much lower densities) and their inhabitants rehoused by the public authority in outer 'overspill' estates (e.g. Kirkby, Scharnhorst), second, voluntary migrations by occupants of private accomodation to better houses and a better physical and social environment in the greener more open areas of the suburbs.

Both of these (non-voluntary, public, voluntary, private) types of decentralisation cause two sorts of problems which we can interpret in the two sides of a coin. Firstly the outmigration is to a large extent selective in that it is the more able, skilled and better paid who can afford to move out, to some extent related to the differential job opportunities as the inner areas' jobs decline compared with the outer areas. The net result is the physical dereliction as 'slums' are cleared (and sometimes not replaced), as factories, pits and warehouses close, and the social deprivation as the very young, the old, the unskilled, the ethnic minorities, the unemployed, the sick and disabled are left behind in the 'Inner City' that symbol of the urban condition of recent years. The erosion of the financial base (the 'rates' or local property taxes in Britain) only serves to exacerbate the problems of public authorities trying to deal with extreme problems of economic, social and physical stresses. We are however well aware that the extent of the problems mentioned, quantitatively as well as qualitatively considerably differs in both regions. The development of 'slums' in the Ruhrgebiet for example is, compared to Merseyside, restricted to a few areas of the city only.

Secondly (on the other side of the coin) the decentralisation produces contrasted problems in the suburbs. Here there are severe problems of demand—for more schools, shops, recreation, for more transport infrastructure or transport provision of a difficult and uneconomic dispersed pattern. The unbalanced demographic structure which contains disproportionate numbers of school children and young adults places further strains on several social provisions especially since they are called upon to provide for a succession of demographic 'waves and troughs'. The dispersed and scattered physical pattern of much of the suburban development, a result of the national housing policies and ownership orientated housing demands, makes it very difficult to achieve any economies of scale in the provision of public sector or private sector facilities.

Although these geographical patterns do show remarkable broad similarities between Merseyside and the Ruhrgebiet as other research would lead us to expect there are one or two points of detailed differences. In the British case the actual physical outcomes of decentralisation appear to be more orderly and less dispersed than in the German case. This may well be explained by the more strategic span of control of British planning powers but other factors may well be at work and this set of differences is worthy of some detailed study.

In both the Ruhrgebiet and Merseyside therefore, the broad patterns of spatial restructuring are strikingly similar and in both cases too, the state (at both regional/county/Land/level and at more local levels) has been put under increasing pressures caused by a declining resource base but escalating problems in the older cores and increased demands for infrastructure and services in the spatially complex but more prosperous suburbs and urban communities of the outer edge of the agglomeration.

THEORETICAL AND METHODOLOGICAL ISSUES OF THE MAIN PROJECT

Whilst the Pilot Project found that the two regions show a common set of broadly defined problems, a review of policies adopted suggested some considerable differences between the two countries. At the most obvious level British regional policy is orientated towards areas like Merseyside, whilst in Germany most of the Ruhrgebiet does not yet benefit from similar Federal policies; these are still orientated towards stimulating development in rural, mainly peripheral, areas. However, it is significant that the current problems of the Ruhrgebiet have led to some political pressure being applied to ensure the region receives more attention; such moves are being made just as this type of policy is being questioned in Britain. This presents an obvious case of the need to learn from each other's experience.

Apparent differences in policy response between Britain and Germany could be hypothesised to result from four factors:

Firstly, the differing economic strengths of the two countries may be significant, with Germany performing better in terms of growth of GNP, the rate of inflation and balance of payments. As well as explaining different policy responses, differences in economic strength could also be an *effect* of different types of policy response.

Secondly, apparent differences in the political and economic philosophy must play their part, with Germany being rather more committed to the competition of the market.

Thirdly, Germany has a more decentralised and diffuse pattern of political power than in Britain. The Federal system, together with the relatively greater power of the local authorities to respond more positively to local needs, though a trend towards greater centralisation of decisions and financial means does seem to be developing.

Lastly, it may be that there is in Germany a more ready acceptance of change by the state system, by the public at large and within the various interest groups such as the Trade Unions.

The Main Project will examine the extent to which these factors have influenced policy, public authority attitudes and the effectiveness of policy. In throwing up apparent differences between Britain and Germany the Pilot Project did, however, lead to a codification of those areas in which differences (or similarities) could be expected to be of *significance* to people living in both societies.

Apart from the necessary academic and scientific achievements of the Pilot Project it has to be stressed again that the personal communication and contacts during the whole Pilot Projects phase were an indispensable precondition for the research work in the Main Project.

Three large areas of work from the main components of the Main Project as a whole. These are:

(i) economic decline and the state's responses;
(ii) urban (spatial) restructuring and the state's responses;
(iii) community responses to both economic decline and urban restructuring.

The simplest way of explaining the content of the project and the 'state of play' is to discuss these three components in the context of the theoretical and methodological issues of the project.

Theoretical and Methodological Issues

Economic decline

During long discussions for the accomplishment of a common understanding of the ways and means to analyze economic decline within the two study regions it had been agreed that:

(i) a central question of the project concerned the comparative analysis of how economic structural change of a region was actually managed;
(ii) such change has primarily to be seen in connection with capital accumulation and associated concentration and centralisation in the context of overall economic and social development;
(iii) a study of the interacting roles of three main actors—capital, the state and the community—would be essential to the comparative analysis.

Besides case studies conducted within the theoretical frameworks of the project to empirically support and prove the hypothesis a full range of back-ground work will be done.

In addition, studies of the principal actor—capital, state and community—will emphasise their dynamic interactions over time. For this a historical approach will be adopted, in the context of which a careful analysis not only of the specific interactions of the actors behaviour *per se* but also of the context within which those actions were placed, will be made.

Case studies will play an essential role for the empirical validation of the analysis. They will focus on selected firms being typical examples for the demonstration of the development, the process and the effects of structural economic change in old industrial regions. The firms are selected out of sectors which are either strongly affected by rationalization processes, redundancies or real or threatening closures or which are, in one way or the other, supported by government programmes to provide new jobs.

The case studies will be performed within a theoretical framework which deals with:

(i) the role of the state in old industrial countries such as Britain and West Germany.
(ii) the accumulation of industry or labour force orientated communal investments;
(iii) the role, the firm (or the branch) plays in the local political context.

In connection with the theoretical framework mentioned above it will become important to define more precise and detailed hypothesis on the reactions of the various actors, hypothesis which will relate to the more general issues identified in the Pilot Project. This will help to ensure that the case studies do not become more narrative but are actually used to illuminate the hypothesis concerning the dynamics of capital, state and community in both the Ruhrgebiet and Merseyside.

Urban restructuring

The major aims of this component of the Ruhr-Mersey Project are:

(i) to make a comparative analysis of the nature and the effects of urban restructuring in each country/region;
(ii) to examine and compare the nature of public policy responses to urban restructuring.

Questions arising in dealing with the problems of urban restructuring in both regions are:

How do economic conditions influence the scope and extent for dealing with such problems?

Does economic growth imply a better quality of life?

Have institutional and cultural traditions led to opportunities or to constraints on solving the negative impacts of urban restructuring?

Are there marked differences of spate intervention between Britain and Germany concerning policies for the accomplishment of problems of urban restructuring?

For several reasons it is neither possible nor desirable to seek for a unique theoretical framework within which to carry out the research. The aims of the study to be undertaken are modest particularly concerning the possibilities for development of theories of urban restructuring. It is felt to be more realistic to look for a careful comparative analysis of possible alternative ways of coping with problems, for possible solutions and for a careful description and explanation of the major similarities and differences.

The body of empirical data derived of the case studies in both regions and the necessary background investigations will be used to evaluate a limited number of alternative theoretical frameworks which others have set up in order to try to explain processes of urban growth, decline and restructuring.

Whilst a great deal of study and analysis will necessarily be directed to 'urban restructuring' in a general sense it will have to be focussed on certain ways. These are fourfold:

—by selecting certain *aspects* of the treating of restructuring viz its *nature*, its impact on the *quality of life* and the *related responses* of public authorities;
—by selecting *housing, education and shopping* for special attentions;
—by assessing the role of the urban land market as a decisive underlying force;
—by the use of *case studies* to illuminate the interaction of the above elements.

The research work on urban restructuring will consist of four strands:

Firstly, to look at the effects of population decline on public policymaking, using quantitative as well as qualitative data and information;
Secondly, a record and analysis will be made of changes in the quality of housing, education and shopping but also with respect to a wider set of indicators (e.g. health, safety, wealth etc.);
Thirdly, to look into the questions of land availability, land market and urban land policies, highly sensitive issues in old industrial regions.
Fourth, to identify the community's own perceptions of changes in the quality of life within the context of the 'community responses' to be analysed in the project.

The effects of population decline will be analyzed by taking four major propositions:

(i) that the need for community services does not necessarily fall in proportion to total population size;
(ii) that the number of necessary skilled professionals may fall faster than the level of need;
(iii) that changing demographic structure may aggravate problems;
(iv) that total resources provided may be reduced in the face of adverse economic conditions.

The focus on housing, education and shopping has several reasons:

(v) *Housing* is the most important item of private consumption (apart from food) in both economies. It is also a field of considerable political debate and private capital accumulation. The nature of the interaction is very different in each country.
(vi) *Education* is (largely) a publicly provided community service and has been chosen because of its relatively

simple policy structure and close relationship to demographic matters.

(vii) *Shopping* represents a services almost entirely controlled by market forces, closely related to population and economic variables and relatively free from government intervention.

The land issue is selected as it draws attention to a policy area, which plays a major role in the process of improving the physical environment of the population in old industrial regions and for the provision of new jobs within the already built-up urban areas. Apart from the general aspects of land ownerships and land speculation in capitalistic society, the problem of unused, underused or misused urban land or the problems of finding new attractive and feasible uses for former industrial land in the context of economic decline and urban restructuring will be investigated.

To tackle the theoretical and methodological problems of urban restructuring case studies will be used. They will help to illuminate the general issues, to trace the dynamics of the interactions between the principal actors and to provide finer-grain data for the evaluation of hypotheses. From the general findings of the Pilot Project the need to select three major case studies in each region became obvious to be representative of:

(i) inner area decline and the preponderance of older private housing;

(ii) outer area growth and the role of public (or semi-public) development;

(iii) inner area improvement by the transformation of former industrial land and the role of the actors involved.

The essence of this area of work is based on firmly agreed aims about methodology and the type and role of case studies. It is further based on an approach which is not rooted in any single clear theoretical perspective but is rather a more exploratory hypothesis rating and refining approach. There is clear agreement to test hypothesis as among others:

(i) that social polarisation in urban areas of old industrial regions is increasing;

(ii) that the working class areas experience difficulty in further improving or even maintaining their quality of life;

(iii) that the actors involved behave in basically the same way in both Merseyside and the Ruhrgebiet.

The integrated research approach will ensure an utmost cross-relation of studies:

(iv) by drawing attention to the spatial environmental aspects and impacts when carrying out the case studies on economic decline.

(v) by incorporating the historical analysis of the role of the state in the investigations on urban restructuring.

Community responses

This aspect of the whole RUHR-MERSEY project is integrative in two important ways. First, it studies the community's responses to both economic decline *and* urban restructuring and is thus a most valuable bridge between the two major streams of work produced. Secondly, it is also designed so as to carry out comparative work in both Merseyside and the Ruhrgebiet.

This stream of work will embody most of the project's concern to understand and evaluate questions of how the 'quality of life' is affected by economic and spatial changes. In addition to trying to form some kind of 'objective' analysis of such changes by the use of certain relatively quantitative indicators, it will also include major studies of a more 'subjective' nature, focussed on how individuals and groups actually themselves *perceive* the quality of life changing around them.

The work will also be concerned with the way in which the community has responded to such changes. It will look at both 'articulated' responses, e.g. those actually voiced by organized groups (typically trade unions, tenents' associations, community groups, political parties etc.) and also at 'non-articulated' responses such as those revealed by social surveys and other more informal types of investigations which could reveal what people have perceived but not expressed.

An important link with the other streams of the project is that all the detailed fieldwork will be carried out in the same case-study areas (see above) and considerable effort will be devoted to understanding individual and group responses to changes in the nature of the work, housing, education etc. Once again it will be important to study not only the articulated responses (of e.g. the Trade Unions) but also the non-articulated viewers which can only be revealed by careful and sensitive interviewing.

EIGHT

HARALD BODENSCHATZ, VOLKER HEISE AND
JOCHEN KORFMACHER

SOME REMARKS TO THE METHODOLOGICAL PROBLEMS OF INTERNATIONAL COMPARATIVE STUDIES ON RESIDENTS' RESISTANCE IN URBAN RENEWAL

RESIDENTS' resistance in an international comparison—what is meant by this? The usual practice of using a foreign country as an example is well known: One analyses the lack of participation in one's own country very often as an inappropriate legal procedure, looks for apparently more advanced methods, parhaps finds them, and advocates them as the latest wonder-cures. In the appraisal of foreign examples the problem of residents' resistance (limited to citizens' participation) is too often separated from the national and local political and economic context, cleanly stripped of contradiction and conflict and presented as a shining model. In this way a political problem is reduced to an organisational procedure; legal acts, forms of organisation and the manner of approach dominate the transferred content.

A critique of idealistic comparative studies is in many ways much easier than the realisation of our own methodological intention to understand the importance of residents' resistance in its polit-economical context, to grasp its local dimensions and to categorize in phases the most important stages of their historical development (i.e. to "periodise" the development of the effected residents' protest in relation to economic and political circumstances on both local and national levels and to

Paper presented at the European Meeting on Applied Urban Research, 1981.

consider the effects of protest and resistance an local policies). The whole effort has to be viewed as an attempt not only to stimulate scientific discussion but to feed back experience to the normal every-day practice of residents' resistance.

In order to carry out local case-studies on the chosen topic in West Berlin, Amsterdam, Roterdam, and London it was essential to design a common research guideline. This was particularly necessary because the field work was to be done by experts out of those cities, familiar with the situation in the case study area, possibly working with or within the local action groups. In order to be of use this guideline had, on the one hand, to guarantee the transposition of the chosen complex of issues—from the theoretical hypothesis to the empirical level—without being, on the other hand, too closely knit—thus methodologically ensuring that the peculiarities of each case (which could not be anticipated from us in advance) are taken into account. Looking at similarities should not a priori lead to differences being ignored; that knowledge is essential for an effective "learning from abroad" and for comparative discussion. Furthermore, this research guideline must categorize in phases the historical development of local resistance, without selecting the criteria for this phases at random, i.e., these criteria should not be too narrow to ensure again that the economic and political changes can be recognized.

In the context of a committed analysis of conflicts in urban policies and the organisation of urban renewal this meant: When considering the national context we had to focus epecially on the change to an austerity policy and its particular effects on housing and renewal policies, mainly describable as "liberalisation" and "recommodification" of social housing against the background of increasing unemployment and decreasing wage incomes. In the local context we had to define the "power-block" with regard to urban renewal (components of the block, dominant type of renewal, ideological legitimation, resources available, etc.). In addition to that we had to examine the opportunities of this block to make concessions within the general framework of citizens' participation. Furthermore, we had to explain the difficulties of the deficit-spending policy resulting mainly from a socialist tradition of housing policy. Finally, we had to establish the type of the urban social movements, as well as their emergence, resulting from a qualitative change of citizens' participation to clarify the process from "social base" to "Social force." In order to categorize their development in phases we chose as relevant turning point: The qualitative change of residents' resistance in terms of programs, forms of resistance—legal or direct action—, and their social base. Those changes normally coincided with the gradual change of the dominant type of urban renewal—slum clearance and redevelopment, rehabilitation, maintenance and repair—mainly due to the effects of the austerity policy.

The definition of the dominant "powerblock" with regards to urban renewal in England and the Netherlands has to consider the tradition of a socialist housing policy of the working class parties in those countries (labour Party, partij van de Arbeid) which in West Germany and West Berlin were unable to recover after their destruction by the Nazi before the second World War. The housing stock in England and the Netherlands comprises of a considerable quantity of council-owned flats and the social housing associations are much more subject to social and political control than in West Germany and West Berlin. In addition to that area approach, urban renewal programs (housing action area, general improvement areas, bouwen voor de buurt) are executed within the responsibility of the local apparatus, large public housing and rehabilitation companies don't exist, who are mainly profit-oriented either for themselves or in close connection with their associated banks.

That is not to say that there are not any "powerblock" in urban renewal which are rather similar to those in West Germany and West Berlin (e.g. capital investment companies, building industry and their various political interlacings with the local state). The important difference lies in the fact that housing policy and working class living area improvement in England and the Netherlands—as far as they are determined by the above mentioned parties—attempt to avoid the speculative increase of land value to a large extent at least in those areas. This creates different political conditions for residents' resistance and for the urban social movement as far as it is related to the provision of housing.

The target of protest and demands from residents is nevertheless the local apparatus in England and the Netherlands, too, because it is obviously responsible for a policy, which passes a major part of housing cost onto the directly effected household in times of hardening austerity policy. Insisting on a local housing provision by municipalisation, without being able to provide sufficient funds for successive rehabilitation, worsens the housing situation at least for a short period and generates residents' resistance. At the same time, there is a tendency to form an alliance with (at least) the left wing of the socialist-social-democratic parties in regard to the demands for appropriate subsidies for housing and urban renewal policies. This difference—compared with the situation in West Germany and West Berlin—is quite fundamental because it provides the residents' resistance directly with the opportunity of institutionalisation within the traditional form of political opposition, thereby contributing a lot to their political force. At the same time, those forms articulated somewhat below the institutional accepted level of political opposition are regarded with scepticism by the traditional working class parties as well as by socialist housing politicians—mainly due to the inherent refusal to allow basic-democratic and grass-rooted resistance to influence local policies effectively—except "smoothing" the intended procedures.

This is particularly true for the squatter movements in England, the Netherlands and in West Berlin which are often portrayed in a bad light by social democratic and/or socialist parties (as well as by the overwhelming part of the trade unions) often with the same arguments as are used by conservatives and reactionary parties and groups (confiscation of flats for the needy, disturbing and blocking urban renewal programs, risking jobs in the building industries, etc.). Legalized forms for self-help by squatters as well as all forms of housing co-operatives (including shortlife, co-ops) are—if not regarded as part of the "liberalisation" process of housing in terms of new "slum landlordism"—

considered mainly as provisional solutions against the background of scarces public expenditure instead of being looked upon as a self-determined housing provision alternative to existing tenures.

These general reflections are based on the outcomings of the local case studies in the various cities. To carry them out, we had to consider not only conceptual but organisational problems. The research fund available was rather inadequate for a proper honorarium for the foreign colleagues who worked for us on a contract—on-each-case-study. The feed-back during the field work, therefore, was as insufficient as the desired cross-co-ordination between the authors themselves and the main research groups. In addition, all the case studies could not be done parallel to each other in the same period of time but only displaced and delayed as well. Due to these reasons and in spite oi the identical research guideline, the actual research procedure varied enormously. Particular because of the necessary consideration of a complex political context categorized in phases and because of the interdisciplinary approach, the different political points of view and different methodological backgrounds of the authors of the various case studies evoked additional problems when sufficient co-ordination and technical organisation are difficult to ensure.

NINE

DAVID C. THRONS

COMMENT OF TOPIC OF THE INTERNATIONALISATION OF URBAN PROBLEMS

Comparing Convergent International Trends*

THE ISSUE of whether cities in all Western societies are converging into a common path of urbanisation has been a central question taken up in the 'post-industrial' society debate. However such arguments ignore the fact that although there may exist similar patterns and problems, the origins of the structures which have produced the urban effects are different. Further, much of the evidence that has been used to support arguments about convergence has been drawn from too narrow a range of countries and too limited a time span (Giddens 1974).

Arguments regarding 'post-industrial' societies focus upon the nature of technology as the determining factor shaping the form of urban structure. This emphasis tends to ignore the vital role played by those who possess economic and political power in shaping how technology is used and how cities will be structured (Konrad and Szelenyi 1977). An approach emphasising these themes will be focussed around not technology but power, class formation and conflict, and the categories of society which will be used are those not of 'industrial' and 'post-industrial' but of capitalist and socialist (Giddens 1974). Within these general categories a further distinction can be made as to whether the societies are of a 'core' or 'peripheral' nature. Such a distinction will serve to indicate the role the country plays

*Paper presented at the European Meeting on Applied Urban Research, 1981.

within the international division of Labour (Wheelright 1980), and this in turn has consequences for the function of the cities within the societies.

In this second type of approach focussing upon the economic, political and social organisation of nation states and their role within the world economy, Australia and New Zealand take on a particular significance. This is because they are societies in which the nature of capitalist development has been quite different from that followed in Western Europe. Thus it contains a number of features not found within the Western European pattern. This factor points to the necessity to analyse urbanisation within a comparative and historical framework (Thorns 1980). It also further points to the dangers of the sometimes simplistic assumptions that are made about the nature of convergence. This is particularly the case where these assertions are made simply on the basis of aggregate statistical data without any recourse to detailed historical analyses. Without a detailed analysis of the development through time of the urban structure, the social and economic processes which were important in shaping the pattern of urban development will often be overlooked or insufficiently recognised.

Australia and New Zealand are not 'core' nations within the world capitalist system nor are they truly 'peripheral' as they do possess a relatively high standard of living and an increasingly sophisticated corporate based capitalist economy. They do, however, depend much more heavily than the 'core' nations upon the export of *primary* products and have a relatively underdeveloped manufacturing sector. Armstrong and Ehrensaft have solved this locational problem by terming Australia and New Zealand along with Canada and Uruguay 'Dominion capitalist Societies' (Ehrensaft and Armstrong, 1978). Dominion capitalist societies are ones which share a common colonial origin and whose economies develop primarily to fulfil the needs of the European, traditionally British, economy for food and raw materials (e.g. mineral wealth). This pattern of development has resulted in the economies of the two countries being narrowly based around a set of primary 'staple' products (meat, wool, dairy produce). This has given a particular importance within these societies to those groups involved in agricultural production and marketing. For example, to farmers and landowners, the servicing industry (stock and stations agents and banking) the agricultural processing industry (meat and dairy works) and lastly to transport services (including shipping). These areas of the economy of both countries have been ones which have experienced a heavy penetration of foreign capital and ownership. For example, in New Zealand, of the five trading banks only one is new Zealand owned. The class structure produced, therefore, in these societies is not one which reflects industrial production with an industrialised bourgeoise and proletariat, but a system which gives prominence to landowners and producers, financiers and exporters. The working class was slow to evolve because of the relatively small proportion employed in manufacturing from the establishment of the pastoral dominance through to the late 1930s. New Zealand, for example, in 1920 had only 22 per cent of the workforce employed in manufacturing, construction and mining and this had only risen to 24 per cent by the mid 1930s. Industrial production was largely related to agricultural processing and was located mainly in small factories mostly in country towns. This pattern only changed as a result of the 1930s depressions, the import substitution policies of the post-1939 period and the rise of the welfare state from 1937 onwards in the New Zealand case. In the most recent decades there have been moves to rationalise agricultural processing with the emergence of much larger production units. They are, however, still rural based rather than in the main urban centres.

Although, therefore, urbanisation, as measured in terms of the proportion of the population in settlements of more than 1000 persons, has traditionally been high, the rural areas have primarily been service rather than manufacturing centres. The cities of the two countries thus did not initially form the setting for economic activity or the wealth base of the countries, they were rather the administrative and service centres. The cities have through time become more important as areas of employment, particularly post-1930s with the shifts into manufacturing and the growth of state sponsored welfare services.

This pattern of urban growth has meant the cities are vulnerable to changes in the level of economic activity and the directions of growth. Since the end of the 1960s both countries have been undertaking "Re-structuring" within their respective economies which has led to a reduced level of demand for domestic production. Thus those employers who developed their operations during the import substitution period for the domestic market have been particularly effected. They are urban-based. Similarly the contraction of state welfare provisions and services has had a most significant impact upon the cities. For example, Canberra's growth has been significantly affected by the Fraser Government's public expenditure reductions. Recent re-structuring has thus brought with it rising urban unemployment within those cities and states (in Australia) not involved in the renewed emphasis upon primary production, and the mining boom or energy projects. These re-directions within the economy are having far reaching effects upon the Australian and New Zealand cities (Stillwell 1980; McDermott 1981).

This brief look at the pattern of New Zealand and Australian city structure and development suggests that this is not purely the product of technology but of social and economic changes. These changes have resulted from the place New Zealand and Australia have occupied within the world system and from the response adopted to the 'crises' the societies have faced this century. The coalitions of class interests represented in the ruling elites has changed through time and this has resulted in different responses being made. These varied responses have had major consequences for the pattern and pace for urban development. The most recent period of change has been the one begun in the 1970s, and continuing into the 1980s which has led to the cities in Australia, situated from Adelaide to Newcastle, feeling the impact of the changed emphasis away from manufacturing to the extraction and export of the mineral wealth of Western Australia and Queensland. Thus population movements have occurred and with them shifts of political and economic power to the boom areas and the growing cities of Perth and Brisbane. In New Zealand the present economic strategy of primary product exporting together with large scale capital intensive energy projects, is having effects upon the regional distribution of employment, wealth and development.

The categories, therefore of 'industrial' and post-industrial of 'convergence' and 'divergence' may well present misleading ones, which serve to divert attention away from the real task of developing accurate historically grounded comparative analyses of urban development. It is only when there are more studies available of this type that it will be possible to adequately assess the extent of convergence or divergence in the paths being followed or urban development within different nation states.

REFERENCES

Ehrensaft P. and Armstrong W., "Dominion Capitalism: A First Statement", *Australia and New Zealand Journal of Sciology*, Vol. 14, 1978.

Giddens A., *The Class Strutcture of the Advanced Societies*, London, 1974

Konrad G. and Szelenyi I., "Social Conflicts of Underurbanisation" in Harloe M. (ed), *Captive Cities*, London, 1977.

McDermott, P., *Develoment Directions for the Canterbury Region.* Canterbury United Council, Christchurch, 1981.

Stillwell, F.J., *Economic Crises Cities and Regions*, Sydney, 1980.

Thorns, D.C. "Problems in the Development of a Comparative Sociological Theory of Urbanisation", *Papers in Urban and Regional Studies*, Vol. 4, 1980.

Wheelright, E.L., "The New International Division of Labour in the Age of the Trans National Corporation', in Willmott, W.E. (ed), *New Zealand and the World: Essays in Honour of Wolfgang Rosenberg*, Christchurch, 1980.

TEN

JOHN D. KASARDA

NEW URBAN POLICIES FOR NEW URBAN REALITIES*

INTRODUCTION

DURING the past two decades, most large metropolitan core cities in North America and Western Europe have simultaneously experienced absolute population losses and substantial declines in their historic employment bases. In the United States, the dispersal of middle-income population and employment opportunities from many core cities has been so substantial that some have begun to question whether these cities, can, or even should, maintain the dominant residential and commercial positions they once held.

In the wake of accelerating dispersion of people and jobs first to the suburbs and now increasingly to nonmetropolitan areas, a number of national urban policies were introduced in the U.S. to lessen the social and economic problems being

*Preparation of this paper was supported, in part, through a contract with the Office of Policy Development and Research, U.S. Department of Housing and Urban Development. Portions are derived from the author's paper, "The Implications of Contemporary Redistribution Trends for National Urban Policy. "*Social Science Quarterly*, Vol. 61 (December, 1980), pp. 373-400.

*Paper presented at the European Meeting on Applied Urban Research, 1981.

experienced by metropolitan core cities and their inhabitants. On the whole, these policies have not succedeed in producing desired results. The reason for this lack of success, in my judgment, rests with the failure of urban policies to give adequate recognition and weight to contemporary technological, economic, and social dynamics underlying the locational decisions of people and firms, the irreversibility of certain spatial trends, and corresponding new roles large cities most effectively perform in advanced service economies.

This paper will examine contemporary spatial trends and their underlying dynamics as they are impacting U.S. cities with the objective of drawing implications for revised urban policies both in the U.S. and abroad. It is my contention that as post-industrial cities structurally transform from centers of production and distribution of material goods to centres of administration, information exchange and higher-order service provision, they are exhibiting new competitive strengths which revised urban policies must recognize and build upon. The future economic prosperity of post-industrial cities rests on enhancing their new service sector roles while providing their structurally unemployed residents with marketable skills and access to jobs.

URBAN TRANSFORMATIONS IN THE TWENTIETH CENTURY

Cities, we know, perform many valuable functions for their national economies and resident populations, However, changing technological and industrial conditions (both nationally and internationally) cause these functions to change over time. In this regard, it must be remembered that nearly all of the largest and most densely settled cities in America and Western Europe developed during a transportation and industrial era that no longer pertains. During this era, cities possessed comparative advantages over other locations that substantially reduced the costs and raised the efficiency of firms concentrating in the cities. These included (a) superior long-distance transportation and terminal facilities; (b) an abundance of labor with skill levels appropriate to industrial needs; (c) agglomeration and mutual-scale economies of nearby complementary businesses;

and (d) a ready availability of externally provided public services such as running water and, later, electricity.

Primitive short-distance transportation technologies and massive manpower needs of America's and Western Europe's rapidly expanding manufacturing economies during the 19th century generated unprecedented concentrative urbanization. Chicago, for example, which was incorporated in 1833 with a resident population of 4,100, grew to over two million residents by 1910—the vast bulk of whom worked and resided within a three mile radius of the city's center. Numerous other industrial cities that evolved during the 19th century also grew as highly compact agglomerations, serving as both residences and workplaces of millions of unskilled and semi-skilled migrants.

A point that cannot be overemphasized is that employment bases of the industrial cities were characterized by entry-level job *surpluses* compared to the entry-level job *deficits* that characterize their job bases today. In the early industrial cities, the only human skills necessary for employment were a willingness and physical ability to work. It was this abundance of low-skill jobs, with few requisites for entry, that attracted the waves of migrants and offered them a foothold in the urban economy. The rapidly expanding urban job base accompanying national economic growth, in turn, provided ladders of opportunity and social mobility for the migrants, most of whom were escaping areas of economic distress.

During the first three decades of the 20th century, a number of innovations occurred in transportation, communication, and production-distribution technologies that reduced the previous advantages cities held as loci for production processes and made uncongested suburban sites more attractive (e.g., the spread of utilities and hard-surfaced highways, shifts from rail to truck shipping, and assembly line production techniques). By the end of World War II, further advances in transportation and communication technologies all but made the inner cities obsolete as locations for large-scale manufacturing and wholesale establishments. A massive exodus of blue-collar jobs from the cities commenced—an exodus that has continued to the present.

Particularly hard hit by blue-collar job losses have been the larger, older central cities of America's northern industrial heartland that are functionally transforming from centers of manufacturing to centers of administration and higher order services (Kasarda, 1978). Unfortunately, it is precisely these cities that also experienced the largest post-war migration flows of people with education and skills ill-equipped for white-collar administrative, financial, professional, and other "knowledge class" jobs that have partially replaced the blue-collar job losses in the cities. The outcome of this mismatch is increased reverse commuting of central city blue-collar workers to suburban jobs and growing structural unemployment among those lower skilled persons residentially confined to inner city areas abandoned by commerce and industry (Kasarda, 1980).

Attempts to remedy the residence-job opportunity mismatch by attracting larger blue-collar firms back to the central cities have largely failed. Despite incentives contained in present urban policies, most industries providing blue-collar jobs are continuing to shun a central city location. Expensive and difficult to assemble tracts of land, congested streets and highways, higher taxes, local government regulations, trade union restrictions, shortages of manpower with the right skills and problems of employee absenteeism and discipline are the most frequent reasons cited by industrialists for not choosing an inner-city location. Directed by their sixth sense of profit, entrepreneurs of blue-collar industries have sought alternative, more cost-effective sites in the suburbs, exurbs, and nonmetropolitan areas which are far better suited to today's advanced transportation and production technologies and which avoid what have become some serious negative externalities of inner-city locations (e.g., high land costs, traffic congestion, and rising crime).

The advantages of decentralized locations

To escape the costs and headaches of a central city location, yet maintain important agglomeration and scale economies, many manufacturers and wholesalers in the U.S. have banded together in modern industrial parks along major suburban and exurban highways. These peripheral industrial parks (over 2,000 of which have formed since 1960) are not only particularly well adapted to advanced production and transportation-distribution technologies but they also generate their own self-contained agglomeration and mutual-scale economies (Muller, 1976). More specifically, they offer ample, relatively inexpensive space for employee parking, freight transfer and automated single-storey production and distribution facilities, as well as excellent accessibility to regional and national markets via interconnecting expressways, beltways, and interstate highways. Information, material, and personnel can be quickly and conveniently transferred between and among proximate plants, and by pooling the costs of security, public utilities, insurance and taxes, mutual-scale economies are obtained that lower the expenses of the individual firms and improve their competitive positions. The decentralized industrial parks provide explicit testimony that agglomeration and mutual-scale economies have, themselves, become footloose, allowing firms to locate almost anywhere in the metropolitan region and beyond.

Further testimony that agglomeration and mutual-scale economies are no longer tied to central locations can be found in the remarkable growth of suburban shopping centers and regional malls in the U.S. during the past 25 years. Between 1954 and 1978, more than 15,000 shopping centres and malls were constructed to serve the expanding middle- and upper-income suburban and exurban populations. By 1975, these shopping centres and malls produced over one-half of the annual retail sales in the United States (Muller, 1976).

Advances in transportation and communication technologies have not only reduced the economies of centrality in older, slower-growth manufacturing, wholesales, and retail industries, but they have also impacted on economies of location in the newer, rapid growth administrative office and research and development sectors. The quintessential feature of the emerging footloose economy in the U.S. may be observed in the substantial development during the past two decades of expansive, style-setting administrative office and research parks in deconcentrated suburban and exurban settings. The telecommunication revolution, in particular, has almost entirely removed the advantages of concentrated centrality for many administrative office and research and development functions. For those firms that must maintain regular contact with other persons or units located either in the central cities or outlying areas, conference picture phones, two-way cable TV, rapid facsimile teleletters and computerized information transmission networks allow a substitution of efficient, high-speed electronic interaction for often time-consuming personal gatherings (Muller, 1976; Hiltz and Turoff, 1978).

Like many ultramodern industrial parks, quite a few of the decentralized office and research parks are located in bucolic, campus-like settings complete with executive clubs, restaurants, swimming pools, tennis courts, jogging tracks, and other amenities attractive to contemporary, more leisure-oriented life-styles. Moreover, since most executives, middle managers, and professionals currently reside in the suburbs and exurbs (by preference recall), the decentralized office and research complexes actually cut residence-to-work place commuting time, energy use and expense. Organizational cost-effectiveness is enhanced by the large, relatively well-educated suburban clerical pool who are eager to work in nearby office complexes at lower wages than they would require if they had to commute to offices in the central cities. Further organizational cost-effectiveness is provided by lower land costs, office rents and taxes, and by substantially lower levels of employee turnover and absenteeism compared with their counterparts in the central cities (Muller, 1976). The interaction of these social, demographic and economic forces would seem to assure that the suburbs and exurbs will far outpace the central cities in white-collar job growth during the 1980s.

The realities of the urban renaissance

This is not to say, however, that there will not be significant central city job growth in white-collar office and professional functions, particularly in those financial, managerial, professional and "knowledge class" occupations that require a substantial amount of quick, nonroutine face-to-face interaction. We can also expect central city employment growth in administrative headquarters offices which continuously utilize diverse sets of external support services such as advertising and public relations; printing and publishing; and legal, accounting, and management consulting services. There are still important economies of proximity for many of these activities, and those who perform them can be stacked one upon another, layer after layer, in downtown office buildings, with relatively little loss of productivity (Porter, 1976).

There is another extremely high-growth industry in older, larger central cities that has received little scholarly inquiry. That is the dramatic rise in convention and tourism business fostered by the growing number of professional and trade associations and rising incomes of a sizable and geographically fluid segment of the national and international population. This rich potential for cities will be commented upon shortly.

First, however, I'd like to comment on the so-called back-to-the-city movement in the U.S. and the purported urban residential renaissance. A number of publications, mostly impressionistic and journalistic in nature and supported by few actual facts have suggested that white, middle class suburbanites are streaming back to inner city neighbourhoods, and that cities are showing remarkable new signs of residential and economic health. Unfortunately, carefully conducted demographic surveys and research on recent residential and employment changes in central cities as a whole lead to more cautious conclusions. The main findings of these surveys and research are as follows:

1. The overwhelming flow of middle class households during the 1970s has been out of, not into, the central cities. For every household with income levels of $15,000 or more who entered central cities during the late 1970s, three such households left the cities. During this period, four out of five family heads who left the central cities had incomes over $15,000 per annum.

2. Revitalization has affected only a small portion of any city's housing stock. Between 1968 and 1978, only one-half of 1 per cent of the nearly 20 million housing units in cities have been affected by revitalization or restoration efforts (U.S. Department of Housing and Urban Development, 1979).

3. The vast majority (more than 70 per cent) of households residing in revitalized central city units were intracity movers and not suburbanites or nonmetropolitan residents who moved back to the city (James, 1980).

4. The concentration of minorities and poverty-level population in central cities is continuing to increase, both in absolute

and proportional terms. Between 1970 and 1980 central cities lost approximately four million white residents, whereas the black population in the central cities increased by more than 1.6 million. Despite a net national decline of 2.2 million persons below the poverty level between 1970 and 1978, the total number of central city residents below the poverty level and dependent on welfare continued its dramatic growth.

5. Substantial residential and commercial disinvestment continues to be active in almost all older, larger central cities, and far exceeds reinvestment. During the 1970s, the expansion of blighted neighborhoods and increase in residential abandonment that characterized these cities were matched with accelerated deterioration and abandonment of commercial and industrial facilities (Sternlieb and Hughes, 1979.)

6. The growth of office employment in the central business districts during the 1970s has not nearly compensated for central city losses of manufacturing jobs and employment declines in the retail and wholesale sectors. As a result, the overall employment base of most large cities is continuing to deteriorate. In New York City, for example, although white-collar professional, clerical and managerial jobs were expanding in Manhattan during the 1970s, New York City as a whole lost more than 600,000 jobs. It has been estimated that this net job loss alone resulted in a tax loss to New York City of almost $500 million annually.

In sum, many major U.S. cities are still in deep trouble as their overall residential and employment bases continue to weaken. This is especially the case for the large, older central cities in the Northeast and North Central regions of the country. In these regions, the forces of counterurbanization are so strong that it is unlikely that any National Urban Policy that would be economically and politically feasible at this time could reverse them, or even substantially slow them down. Nevertheless, based on what we can learn from contemporary spatial redistribution trends and their underlying technological, economic, and social forces, a number of implications for National Urban Policy can be drawn.

From continuing population deconcentration and suburban sprawl
Policy makers should no longer necessarily assume that dispersion is bad and concentration is good in terms of relative social, economic, and environmental costs and benefits. By dispersing from the central cities, tens of millions of Americans and Europeans have been able to improve their housing, employment conditions and living environments. *Sprawl*, in fact, is a loaded term, full of pejorative connotations. Despite the conventional wisdom of many city planners and academics labeling suburban and exurban growth as haphazard, inefficient, and undesirable, new research is demonstrating that peripheral growth is not nearly as inefficient or undesirable as once believed. Without the guidance of any conscious master design, the suburbs and exurbs in the U.S. are evolving their own relatively self-sufficient hierarchy of activity centers, ranging from higher-order regional commercial and employment centers to lower-order convenience goods and residential centers (Muller, 1976). The evolution of this multifunctional, nested hierarchy of activity centers has given rise to a new form of spatial organization—the polycentric ecological field—which has replaced the technologically antiquated primate structure of the monocentered industrial metropolis. Within this new, more diffuse form of spatial organization, the traditional metropolitan central business district has become just one specialized node in a multinodal, multiconnective ecological field of interdependent activity centers, extending outward as far as 100 miles from the metropolitan core. The fact that the cost-effectiveness and productivity of many modern economic activities are enhanced in outlying nodes has made them valuable job generator for the U.S. economy. Moreover, as outlying activity centers have grown, they have begun to develop their own nearby labour sheds, reducing employee commuting distances and thus daily travel expenses. Polycentric nodes also reduce problems of convergence, congestion, air pollution and wear and tear on core infrastructure (i.e., streets, highways, bridges) associated with extensive journey-to-work commutation and truck shipments into and out of the traditional monocentered metropolis (Schneider and Noguchi, 1978).

•

In terms of residential energy consumption, large concentrations of high density housing preclude widespread use of steady-state energy sources e.g., solar collectors and windmills). Likewise, greater reliance on replaceable fuels to supplement home heating (such as the use of wood-burning stoves) would create unbearable air quality conditions in larger concentrations. Dispersed, low-density settlements, on the other hand, are able to tap more pragmatically the energy of natural systems as partial replacement of expensive fossil fuels (Vining, 1979). They are also able to drain values directly from the natural environment in panorama, recreational amenities, greenbelts, waste absorption, noise buffers, micro-climate, water quality control, etc. that must be compensated for in large population concentrations by purchased services that raise costs and taxes (Odum et al., 1976).

Large, dense population concentrations, in general, require and/or demand more expensive packages of public services and programs than do smaller, more dispersed communities. Increased demand for (and dependence upon) public services in large population concentrations not only substantially raises government costs, both directly and indrectly, but also makes residents and businesses located in these concentrations more vulnerable to organized actions of public employees (Altschuler, 1977).

From the functional transformation of large cities

National urban policies must clearly recognize that the era of massive, centralized industrialization is over and that large, dense concentrations of people and factories have become technologically obsolete. Urban policies based on the assumption that productivity is enhanced in large urban areas are outdated and wrong, as evidenced by the consistent location decision-making of industrial leaders (McCarthy and Morrison, 1979). No policy will overcome prudent entrepreneurial decisions to locate where costs are minimized and returns maximized.

In this regard, new urban policies should work *with* the forces of spatial redistribution rather than fruitlessly attempting to reverse them. If local policymakers are really serious about revitalizing their urban cores and avoiding future economic stagnation in the central cities, they should cease attempting to entice older production industries back to the central cities, and implement programs to help develop the urban cores in terms of their competitive strengths. Thus, along with continuing to foster the development of administrative, financial, and professional office jobs in the central business districts (CBDs.) the cores of major cities should be revitalized into culturally rich, architecturally exciting magnets for conventions, tourism and leisure-time pursuits of regional, national, and even international populations. All structural indicators point to the office and cultural-leisure service industries as providing the greatest potential for central city economic expansion and job generation over the next two decades. Special efforts should be made to develop central city cores as pedestrian-safe complexes of restaurants, hotels, nightclubs, museums, theaters, sport arenas and other cultural, recreational and entertainment facilities that would attract round-the-clock growth-industry resources to the core, as well as economically and aesthetically complement the increasing number of nine-to-five, high-rise office buildings now beginning to dominate most CBDs. These efforts should include concurrent support for the revitalization and restoration of "close-in" historic neighborhoods, which would both contribute to the cultural appeal of the urban core and provide convenient residences, for a portion of those employed in the CBDs.

From the growing mismatch of the skills of the residential labor force of cities and the types of job opportunities expanding in the city

National urban policies must work to break down the restrictive covenants, zoning regulations and barriers of racial and income housing discrimination that exist near many expanding suburban, exurban and nonmetropolitan blue-collar job bases. Building more public housing the inner cities will likely aggravate the problems of the residence-job opportunity mismatch and ensure that a large portion of their inhabitants remain dependent on the state. Indeed, it is becoming increasingly apparent that some urban-targeted welfare programs may be inadvertently anchoring the disadvantaged in areas of economic distress and, thereby, damaging their longterm economic prospects. Dependent on public housing and place-oriented income and in-kind transfer payments, the disadvantaged cannot easily follow low-skilled jobs that have dispersed from the cities. Discrimination and lack of low-cost housing in many areas of employment growth compound the problem. As a result, a growing urban underclass finds itself increasingly isolated in segregated economic wastelands where there are few prospects for permanent or meaningful employment. New urban policies are required that will help dissolve bonds unintentionally forged between cities and the dependent poor, that help structurally unemployed urban residents acquire the skills necessary to participate in their transforming local economies, as well as assist (rather than hinder) those who desire to migrate to places where jobs appropriate to their skills are still expanding. In my opinion, a thinner central city population composed largely of those who desire to live in the city and have appropriate job opportunities nearby would create a far more vibrant central city than results from present policies that unintentionally warehouse millions of disadvantaged in U.S. cities, to the benefit of neither.

From the incipient "back-to-the-city" neighborhood revitalization movement

Despite the numerous articles in the press describing a "back-to-the-city" movement of the middle class, the predominant flow remains in the opposite direction. Those who are returning from suburbia or freely choosing to remain in U.S. cities are rarely middle-income families with younger children, but single professionals, childless couples with dual incomes, older families whose last son or daughter has left the household, those leading unconventional lifestyles, and others who cherish and can afford the rich cultural amenities, specialized services, and myriad stimuli that downtown living offers. These groups, no doubt, will serve as the primary demographic component of inner-city residential revitalization in the years ahead. For them, the emerging consumption-oriented city provides attractive advantages compared to dispersed, low density, home-centered communities.

Building on emerging city strengths

The principle of comparative advantage also holds the key to the revitalization of future employment bases of major cities in advanced economies. Their economic metamorphosis from centers of material goods production to centers of information exchange and service consumption calls for urban policies that will foster the cities' new rapid growth administrative and higher-order service sector activities. Successful urban policies of the future will work with, rather than attempt to fend off, structural change in cities' economies. Thus, it would be an expensive mistake to attempt to draw (by tax incentives or other means) larger production facilities back to the metropolitan cores or reconstruct the historic employment bases of cities undergoing industrial transformation. On the contrary, national economic prosperity (upon which the health of cities is inextricably dependent) and increasing world-wide economic competition dictate policies that (a) encourage the location of industrial facilities where their overall productivity and cost-effectiveness are maximized and (b) reinforce those sectors of central city economies that have the greatest comparative advantage in the national and world economic order. Instrumental to the latter would be policies that help major cities exploit their unique position as international market and cultural-service nodes to capture increased capital investment and revenue from abroad by attracting multinational corporate offices, international finance complexes, and foreign tourists.

To ease structural unemployment, a revised urban policy should simultaneously facilitate the development of lower- and moderate-income housing near expanding suburban, exurban, and nonmetropolitan job bases and support intensive, up-to-date technical training programs that will provide all those desiring employment with appropriate skills. Recent proposals by some U.S. government officials to subsidize massive numbers of jobs in traditional and marginal employment sectors of central cities and "reindustrialize" older, declining urban industries will do little either to strengthen the competitive economic position of cities or improve long-run employment opportunities for their residents. As implied above, economic advancement of the cities and maximum job creation can best be accomplished through policies that promote urban growth industries whose functions are consistent with the roles computer-age cities most effectively perform. Expeditious development of these industries would not only directly add substantial numbers of new jobs in the cities but it also would have local revenue spin-off and employment multiplier effects that would likely create *far more* jobs in the traditional and marginal sectors of central city economies than could federal subsidies to these sectors. Moreover, the jobs generated through this form of private sector expansion would be relatively self-sustaining and, hence, less vulnerable to the political vicissitudes of public funding.

Revised national urban policies, then, must take an entirely new view of the functions of cities in the post-industrial era and of the triadic relationship among deconcentration, private-sector development and urban economic welfare. They will require programs that are consistent with the redistributional forces of economic development and that address the roots of urban structural unemployment rather than programs that attempt to reverse the paths of development and ameliorate symptoms of underlying employment problems through place-oriented subsidies.

We must have national urban policies that provide for the welfare of those incapable of economic self-sufficiency. Yet, policymakers also must recognize that the long-term economic health of central cities and their inhabitants will be served only through increased private-sector investment and through the relocation and/or appropriate retraining of the structurally unemployed. This implies a fundamental reorientation of national urban policies from emphasizing expensive stopgap programs to counter market and job redistribution trends to emphasizing economic development programs that will stimulate private-sector investment and job expansion and facilitate the relocation and/or retraining of those able to fill the newly generated jobs. As long as national urban policies are dominated by programs that work against, rather than with, the modern forces of change discussed, the policies will fail. In the meantime, they will continue to waste an immense amount of human and fiscal resources and further impede prospects for improved national industrial productivity.

REFERENCES

Altshuler, A., "Review of the Costs of Sprawl", *Journal of the American Institute of Planners*, 43 (April), 1977, 207-209.

Hiltz, S.R. and M. Turoff, *The Network Nation*. Addison-Wesley, Reading, Mass, 1978

James, F.J., "The Revitalization of Older Urban Housing and Neighborhoods." *In The Perspective City* (A.P. Solomon, ed.), pp 130-160. M.I.T. Press, Cambridge, 1980

Kasarda, J.D., "Urbanization, Community, and the Metropolitan Problem." In *Handbook of Contemporary Urban Life* (D. Street and Associates, eds.), 1978, pp 27-57. Jossey-Bass, San Francisco, Cal.

Kasarda, J.D., "The Implications of Contemporary Redistribution Trends for National Urban Policy," *Social Science Quarterly* 61 (December), 1980, 373-400.

McCarthy, K.F. and P.A. Morrison, *The Changing Demographic and Economic Structure of Nonmetropolitan Areas in the United States*. Rand Corporation, Santa Monica, Cal., 1979.

Muller, P.O., *The Outer City*. Resource Paper No. 75-2. Association of American Geographers, Washington, D.C., 1976.

Odum, H., et al., "Net Energy Analysis of Alternatives for the United States." In *Middle and Long-Term Energy Policies and Alternatives*: Volume I, Appendix. Hearing before the Subcommittee on Energy Power of the Committee on Interstate and Foreign Commerce, U.S. House of Representatives. U.S. Government Printing Office, Washington, D.C., 1976.

Porter, P.R., *The Recovery of American Cities*. Two Continents Publishing Group, New York, 1976.

Schneider, J. and T. Noguchi, "The Role of advanced Transit in the Implementation of the Polycentric City Concept," *High Speed Ground Transportation*, 12 (1), 1978, 1-22.

Sternlieb, G. and J.W. Hughes, "New Dimensions of the Urban Crisis." Presented before the Subcommittee on Fiscal and Intergovernmental Policy of the Joint Economic Committee, US.. Congress, March 20. U.S. Government Printing Office, Washington, D.C., 1979.

U.S. Department of Housing and Urban Development, "Wither or Whether Urban Distress." Working paper presented before the Joint Economic Committee, U.S. Congress, March 20. U.S. Government Printing Office, Washington, D.C., 1979.

SECTION TWO

COMPARISON OF NATIONAL AND INTERNATIONAL URBAN RESEARCH

ELEVEN

JACQUES ROBERT

CURRENT RESEARCH TRENDS IN THE EUROPEAN COUNTRIES

Premises for Transnational and Comparative Urban and Regional Research*

INTRODUCTION

COMPARATIVE research is particularly fruitful when it is based upon research concepts and available findings on common topics concerning various countries. It is therefore, of primary importance to know the most perceived problems and the current research priorities in a number of countries.

The most common problem perceived nowadays in the European countries is undoubtedly that important changes in the economic structure as well as in the technologies used are taking place within a context of economic and sometimes of demographic stagnation. It is not the first time that European society has to face important economic and technological changes. The 1950s and the 1960s were also characterised by important changes. But the context was different:

—the changes could find their justification in the economic growth which accompanied them;
—the awareness about possible negative effects of change was much lower;
—practically no organisational unit existed for the

*Paper presented at the European Meeting on Applied Urban Research, 1981.

comprehensive evaluation of the long-term economic, social and environmental impacts of these processes.

We already know that the economic and technological changes of the 1950s and 1960s not only generated benefits as far as the local and regional levels are concerned; they also generated basic problems such as the emergence of an interregional division of labour or serious environmental damage and decline in urban areas.

The early 1970s were characterised by efforts to stress the political nature of the planning process and made the decision-makers and the planning authorities aware of group interests and planning alternatives.

It is precisely the progressive reduction of available resources causing a subsequent reduction of the number of realistic planning alternatives which induces a climate of uncertainty and even of anxiety in the field of urban and regional planning. The impression prevails that a number of economic and technological changes are underway and that not much can be done about their local and regional impacts when these are negative.

The questions addressed to urban and regional researchers are the following:

(i) What is the nature of the changes underway?
(ii) What will be their impact at the regional and urban level?
(iii) How far are these changes inevitable? Is it possible to limit or to adapt them in order to reduce their negative impact?
(iv) Is it possible to conceive alternative development strategies which are able to counterbalance the unfavourable effects of the changes underway?

RESEARCH ON REGIONAL PROBLEMS

General trends

A set of priorities common to several countries can be found in the following fields:

Analysis and anticipation of changes at the regional and interregional level:

(i) Regional impacts of international economic changes and of industrial adjustment on the economic base and on the regional labour market (automation of production, requirements for professional qualification);

(ii) Delineation of declining and relatively prosperous areas;

(iii) Location trends of newly created activities (role of regional, multiregional and multinational enterprises);

(iv) Inter- and intra-regional migration;

(v) Spatial diffusion of know-how and of technological innovation (telecommunication, micro-electronics, etc.);

(vi) Impact of changes on the urban systems of the regions.

Research on the definition of alternative strategies of regional development

—Definition of the strategies, in particular of those based on the promotion of the endogenous potential of the regions (promotion of medium-sized and small enterprises in the field of commercialisation and technical modernisation; promotion of professional training, exploitation of renewable energy sources, etc.);

—Research on instruments necessary to implement these strategies (evaluation of past programmes of regional economic development, proposals for a revision of the system of regional incentives);

—Research on the requirements for the political-administrative framework at the regional level for the implementation of new strategies (regionalisation, devolution of powers in economic planning, competence for the coordination of sectoral policies, etc.).

Selected national examples

As far as trend analyses and anticipative research on the regional impacts of economic and technological changes are concerned, valuable examples can be found in Sweden, France and

Switzerland. The Swedish Expert Group for Research on Regional Development (ERU) is involved in a research programme concerning the regional consequences of the division of labour, of specialisation in the productive activities and of choices in technology. Research projects conducted under the auspices of the Swedish Council for Building Research concern structural changes in industrial and commerce and their impact on communities and employment.

In France, a comprehensive research programme was adopted earlier this year, just before the change of government, and is presently being implemented. It can be considered as a programme of basic research aiming at measuring the local and regional effects of a disturbed economy. In the regional field we find the following priorities: mobility of activities and the labour force after 1974 according to sector categories and professional qualification, relationships between the vulnerability of economic sectors at the national level and the vulnerability of areas specialising in these sectors, location patterns and location factors of newly created enterprises, distribution of these locations through large, medium-sized and small towns, emergence of new types of production, not based on multiregional or multinational enterprises, but, on the contrary, on local initiatives (small firms, home work, etc.). The national research programme on regional problems currently being implemented in Switzerland focusses on the balance of regional labour markets, on interregional migration, on the regional disparities in technology and productivity, on the interregional mobility of know-how, on the spatial mobility of industrial decision-making centres and on regional disparities in the educational system.

Less emphasis is presently being placed on the study of urban systems and urban networks, in particular in relation to the general economic and technological changes. A major study is devoted to the evolution of the national urban system in Switzerland and to its evolution prospects, but it is not sure how far the above-mentioned changes play a significant role in the research approach chosen. A working group of the Committee for Housing, Building and Planning of the Economic

Commission for Europe concluded recently about the evolution of urban networks: 'altogether, the trends concerning the location of manufacturing, services and housing point towards a continuation of recent decentralisation, even if there is considerable variation and if many trends seem contradictory.' As far as research is concerned, the group advocated the elaboration of contrasting alternative distribution patterns of population and activities as undertaken in Denmark and the U.K. and thought that 'calculations like these may be valuable for planners for at least two reasons: they give the limits to the possible changes that planners should be prepared to tackle, and they also give the limits to the networks that planners and politicians can put up as realistic development goals.'

In the field of regional research, the evolution of rural areas seems also to be of common interests for several countries. The Norwegian Institute for Urban and Regional Research has undertaken a project on the problems of areas with a low population density and with small and medium-sized centres. In Sweden, a study was carried out on the planning problems of rural areas in relation to combined forms of employment. A similar topic has also been chosen by the research department of the National Physical Planning Agency of the Netherlands, furthermore, scenerios on possible developments in the agricultural sector are being written in Holland and a study is made about the overlapping of functions in rural areas.

Substantial research on the definition of alternative strategies of regional development has so far been conducted mainly in West-Germany at the federal level, but the interest about this topic is rapidly growing in a number of countries.

In West-Germany, the Federal Minister of Building, Urban and Regional Planning, arguing that less and less must be expected from the inter-regional reallocation of resources, devoted various projects to the mobilisation of the endogenous potential of regions. The strategy advocates the regional adaptation to changing technical and economic conditions by means of the repid adoption of innovations and pays a great deal of attention to the promotion of medium-sized and small enterprises. The outcome of the research suggests that the main problems of small firms in peripheral regions can be found in the area of human capital, information provision, management quality and risk capital and proposes the creation of a multi-functional regional policy system capable to respond quickly and in a flexible way to a variety of functional deficits in a specific area. The debate relates to the revision of the system of regional development incentives, to the creation of new types of intermediary agencies for the application of public policies to private firms and even to the devolution of planning powers to regional bodies representing directly the interests of the regions. This also raises the question of regional identity to which several projects are devoted in Switzerland.

RESEARCH ON URBAN AND METROPOLITAN PROBLEMS

General trends

Analysis and anticipation of changes at the metropolitan and urban level

(i) Local and urban impact of major economic and technological changes (closing down of industrial plants, emergence of new types of activities and of new professions, anticipation of changes in the tertiary activities due to the increased importance of micro-electronics and telecommunication techniques);

(ii) Changes in the structure and distribution pattern of metropolitan and urban employment (location factors, skill requirements, etc.);

(iii) Inner-regional and inner-metropolitan migration, evolution of commuting movements (importance and causes of changes);

(iv) Changes in the structure and distribution pattern of urban services (retailing system);

(v) Changes in the economic and social value of urban and metropolitan spaces;

(vi) Changes in the way of life (evolution of consumption patterns, in particular in relation to the economic recession, recreational mobility, etc.); Role and evolution of accessibility.

Research on urban and metropolitan development strategies

(i) Role of the municipalities in counterbalancing decline, in particular in inner city areas (involvement of local authorities in economic development, provision of services from different groups, urban land policy, housing policy);

(ii) Evolution of the policies of local authorities in a climate of economic uncertainty (importance and character of public policies in relation to the evolution of financial resources at the local level, impact of economic recession on the evolution of local institutions);

(iii) Energy management and local planning (energy saving through urban planning, choice of new technologies, etc);

(iv) Improvement of living environment in urban areas (provision of larger recreational facilities, reduction of traffic disturbances, etc.);

(v) Monitoring and evaluation of public policies (urban renewal, revitalisation, urban transport, citizen involvement, etc.).

Selected national examples

The study of the local impacts of major economic and technological changes forms part of the research programme recently adopted in France: the question asked is why certain towns or metropolitan areas succeed in adapting their economic base and why others do not? Is it possible to identify various types of local economic dynamism?

Various projects concern the anticipation of change. The National Swedish Institute for Building Research has conducted a research project about urban structure and communication techniques, the main purpose of which was to study the potential impact of telecommunication and information technology on urban and rigional structure. A similar project on 'information technology and urban development' is being carried out by the DIFU Institute in Berlin. Research on change in the structure and distribution of metropolitan and urban employment is being carried out in the U.K. and in the Netherlands. The inner cities research programme in Britain focusses on the difficulties experienced by young inner city school leavers when seeking employment, on problems caused by the large-scale transition from manufacturing to service based industry, on the problems faced by the labour force in adjusting to changing employment demands and periods of unemployment as well as on the ability of the construction industry to boost inner cities economies through inner city reconstruction work. In the same context, the British research programme investigates industrial change in urban areas and in particular the factors which influence firms in decisions about expansion and location of premises. The Dutch projects concern the location trends of employment in metropolitan areas, in growth centres and medium-sized towns. Similarly, a project has been conducted in West Germany on structural changes of employment in concentration areas. A better understanding of inner-regional and inner-metropolitan migration processes is a common priority in Britain, the Netherlands, Sweden, Switzerland and West-Germany. The British programme is concentrating upon the attitudes and perceptions of the inner city residents and attempting to link these with actual patterns of behaviour. It pays particular attention to the circumstances surrounding the moves made by in and out migrants as well as to the situation of those who stay in the inner areas and to their perception of constraints restricting their mobility. In Holland, research aims at differentiating the variables linked to housing from those linked to workplace in the choice of residence of the population; it also concerns the migration processes within the metropolitan areas in relation to the urban policies applied.

Changes in the structure and distribution patterns of urban services are being studied particularly in Scandinavian countries. In Norway, various projects concern the provision of community services in urban areas as well as the provision of facilities for special groups of population (aged, handicapped, children). The Swedish projects concentrate on changes in the retailing system, in particular in the conversion of city blocks to large interlinked retailing units containing shops, squares and pedestrian streets as well as on consumer reactions to the closure of small stores in housing areas.

The French research programme focusses on the identification of the factors which contribute to the valorisation or devaluation of urban spaces, that is to say to the changes of their economic and social value. The research attempts to find out how far the economic recession exerts an impact on the process of valorisation/devaluation and what the respective roles of the private sector and of public policies are in this process.

Changes in the way of life and in the behaviour of inhabitants of urban and metropolitan areas are specially taken into account in the French research programme, in particular changes in the consumption and mobility patterns in relation to the economic recession.

The research trends on local public policies in various European countries also reveal a number of similarities. The main question raised is: What can local authorities do to counterbalance urban decline?

Some projects analyse the reactions of the local authorities to the economic recession. In Sweden, a project, aiming to clarify the opportunities of local action in times of crisis and the institutional preconditions for influencing structural change, was devoted to the decision-making process concerning the closing down of steel plants and to its impact on the local economy. The French research programme refers to the analysis of interaction between the public and the private sector in order to define the potential instruments of a local economic policy.

The British inner cities research programme focusses on the scope for local authority involvement in the economic development of its area as well as on the impact and effectiveness of local authority initiatives. A crucial question is the evolution of financial resources of local authorities. The British programme proposed to show how the changing size and composition of inner city populations and the decline and structural change within economic activity can be related to local authority expenditure and revenue. The French programme wishes to explore the evolution of the financial demand at the local level in relation to the increasing number of organised groups and associations, to increasing social problems, etc. It proposes also to explore the impact of the economic recession on the evolution of the local institutions. The questions raised are: how are the new local constraints internalised into the local system of public management? What are the possibilities for adapting the structure and the functions of local administration to different contexts?.

All countries pay a great deal of attention to the question of energy conservation in relation to urban planning. The most important research programmes have been and still are conducted in Sweden and West Germany. The Swedish projects concern energy management as part of long-term physical planning (development of methods and routines for incorporating energy management aspects into long-term urban planning), new energy systems and technology evaluation as part of local authorities' decisionmaking, etc. The German projects focus on integrated local energy systems, relationships between settlement structure and systems of district heating, measures of urban planning to save energy in urban traffic, energy saving in relation to urban renewal, exploitation of renewable energy in relation to spatial planning.

As a follow-up to the research programmes on local decision-making processes, a number of countries (U.K., West Germany) are at present devoting research efforts to the evaluation and monitoring of public policies. This new priority can be explained by the present scarcity of public resources which increases the need for rational utilisation of resources involved in public policies.

ROLE, OPPORTUNITIES AND CONSTRAINTS OF TRANSNATIONAL AND COMPARATIVE RESEARCH

The above-mentioned research topics constitute a consistent catalogue which can be used as a starting point for the formulation of transnational and comparative research. A number of concluding remarks must be formulated:

Transnational and comparative research has a long tradition in Europe. During the past decade numerous comparative studies about planning instruments and planning policies have been carried out. A large number of them omitted to take into account the fact that planning policies and planning instruments are political responses to problem situations which are not at all similar in all countries. A purely instrumental comparative research shows, therefore, a number of shortcomings. Comparative research, in the future, should pay a greater attention to the socio-economic contexts within which urban and regional policies are applied.

In spite of the economic recession and of the general trend towards more policy-oriented research, a number of countries conduct fundamental research on socio-economic processes. This type of research aims at a better understanding of the basic economic and social processes and of their spatial translation. It is quite rare that basic and policy-oriented research are pursued simultaneously with the same intensity in a given country. Transnational comparison of research methods and research outputs can, therefore, benefit from their mutual complementarity.

There are strong interactions between the research method and the content of the research itself. The best example is that of scenario-writing. Scenarios in regional planning were first developed in France after 1968 as an ideological reaction to the traditional forecasting models. They were primarily a means of introducing into forecasts the results of recent fundamental research. Some years later, other countries like West Germany and the Netherlands adopted scenario-writing purely as a new technique which rapidly showed a deficit in fundamental research in these countries and induced greater efforts in this field. The cross-border transfer of research techniques can, therefore, contribute significantly to the improvement of knowledge.

TWELVE

HORST M. BOLTING

EVALUATING URBAN AND REGIONAL RESEARCH IN THE FEDERAL REPUBLIC OF GERMANY*

PRESENT SIGNIFICANCE OF EVALUATION RESEARCH

THE departmental researah of the Federal Ministry for Regional Planning, Building and Urban Development relating to regional planning and urban development has been grouped since 1974 in the medium-term research programme "Regional Planning and Urban Development."[1] The aim of this programme is to obtain instruments and decision-oriented research findings for the areas dealt with by the Ministry and then to translate these findings, where possible, into legislative action or at least use them in preparing legislation. The strong bias of the research programme towards facilitating the preparation of instruments and assisting the decision-making process is one of the chief reasons why an increasingly large proportion of the research projects commissioned during the last few years has been concerned with the impact and success of individual policies and measures.

It is not possible here to deal adequately with the projects which have already been completed or with those currently in progress or with the results of these projects. This paper is concerned with a few—in the author's view—typical aspects and results of the Ministry's evaluation research. For reasons of

*Paper presented at the European Meeting on Applied Urban Research, 1981.

clarity, however, a few basic points about the programme must first be explained. First a word on the scope of the programme in quantitative terms.[2] A total of more than 200 projects involving funds amounting to more than DM 50 million were commissioned during the first eight years. Over 150 projects had already been completed at this stage. The reports of the findings have been published by the Ministry in the majority of cases.

Evaluating research under this programme has gone into almost the complete range of state instruments. Studies have been conducted to determine the impact and effectiveness not only of existing financial support schemes and state infrastructural measures but also of legal regulations. In view of the fact that an important part of the Ministry's work is concerned with co-ordinating the use of regionally significant funds[3] similar measures and programmes adopted by other Ministries and having a regional and environmental impact have also been examined.

Adequate background knowledge and research facilities are prerequisites for research aimed directly at providing advice on a political level. Evaluation research has not yet satisfied these requirements.[4] Thus the material and methodological preconditions which must be fulfilled before concrete evaluation analysis can begin had to be developed first in the majority of cases.[5] For this reason the evaluation research of the Federal Ministry for Regional Planning, Building and Urban Development—in contrast with other research topics—comprises three typical elements:

—preliminary study of methods
—main study or studies
—transfer and utilization of research findings.

POLITICAL APPLICATION OF THE FINDINGS OF EVALUATION RESEARCH

Problems and conclusions

Initial findings of practice-oriented evaluation research in the fields of regional planning and urban development are now available. There is no doubt that this has been a learning process for all concerned and that important progress has already been made. On the other hand there are still a great many scientific, administrative and political problems to be solved and obstacles to be overcome.[6]

The following is not concerned with the findings to date with regard to methods. It is intended rather to concentrate on the problems of translating research findings into policy. The main purpose of practice-oriented evaluation research in the fields of regional planning and urban development is to provide scientific knowledge for the work of the Ministry.[7] In spite of this objective the extent to which research findings are actually implemented cannot, however, be the only yardstick for assessing the "success" of evaluating research. The important thing is to minimize the obstacles to implementation.

It is probably not possible to establish general rules for implementing the findings of evaluation research in the fields of regional planning and urban development. There are a number of reasons for this. These include the differences in the initial political conditions, the intended use to which the findings are to be put or even the quality of the findings themselves. Experience has shown, however, that typical problems arise when the findings of evaluation research are being translated into policy. But these problems can be solved to a certain extent at least.

Two typical basic problems will now be described which have in the past considerably impaired the implementation of the evaluation research of the Federal Ministry for Regional Planning, Building and Urban Development:[8]

—limitations resulting from different methodological approaches (case studies or complex statistical analyses)
—limitations resulting from the conflicting interests of the Ministry on the one hand and those affected on the other

(a) The evaluation analysis commissioned so far by the Federal Ministry for Regional Planning, Building and Urban Development in the fields of regional planning and urban development may roughly divided into two categories: case studies and complex statistical analyses.

Translating the findings into policy has involved problems in both cases. As far as case studies are concerned it is their non-representative character[9] which is objected to while in the case of complex statistical analyses it is the abstract, theoretical and empirical approach which poses problems.[10] Thus each method is criticized for not also having the positive qualities of the other.

Practice-oriented evaluation research therefore faces a dilemma which can only be resolved with great difficulty. With the methodological instruments at its disposal evaluation research can only produce results which are relatively easy to criticize and which can be refuted with simple arguments. What conclusions may be drawn from this?

The improvement of the methodology involved is an urgent task for evaluation research. The aim in this connection should be not so much to refine *one* method as to work towards achieving a synthesis of the different methods.[11] A considerable amount of rethinking is required in this area, particularly on the part of some higher education institutes. It is of no help to practice-oriented evaluation research when different scientific "schools" (who often choose to ignore views from outside their own circles) work side by side but isolated from one another and avoid real discussion wherever possible.[12]

(b) Evaluation research automatically affects a wide range of interests and groups in society. In so far as the findings of evaluation research are translated into policy this generally results in a restructuring of "benefits" and "burdens." This redistribution process invariably produces "winners" and "losers".

This explains the very considerable political problems involved in implementing the findings of evaluation research. Experience to date has shown that these obstacles can be partly and in some cases completely overcome. It has been found, for example, that by involving those affected at an early stage in the process their willingness to accept the findings can be significantly improved. Attempts were therefore made from the very outset to promote close co-operation between the researcher and the local authorities concerned when the impact of the instruments of urban development were being investigated.[13]

The active participation of those affected by the proposed measures does not, of course, guarantee that the translation of the findings into policy will be successful. Conversely it may be said that when no provision is made for early participation the obstacles are much more serious. Efforts are therefore being made in evaluation research in the fields of regional planning and urban development to find suitable ways of encouraging and promoting the co-operation of all persons and groups directly or indirectly affected by the measures concerned.

FUTURE SIGNIFICANCE OF EVALUATION RESEARCH IN THE FIELDS OF REGIONAL PLANNING AND URBAN DEVELOPMENT

Evaluation research already plays an important role in the departmental research commissioned by the Federal Ministry for Regional Planning, Building and Urban Development. Its future significance will be characterized by two conflicting forces: On the one hand the "demand" for evaluation analysis will continue to exist for, among others, the following reasons:

—To successfully co-ordinate measures and programmes the Ministry depends on an adequate supply of information being available.

—The pressure of problems in the areas the Ministry is concerned with is not likely to decrease.

—Given the shortage of public funds available the need for the Ministry to justify its programmes and measures will tend to increase.

On the other hand, however, the continuing demand for evaluation analysis contrasts with formidable and presumably growing resistance on the part of those affected by the measures concerned. This opposition to evaluation research may be explained in the majority of cases by a desire to safeguard existing privileges. At the same time it must be admitted that the present methodological weakness of evaluation research make it relatively easy to criticize its findings. Furthermore, the work of the Ministry is concerned with highly sensitive areas as a result of which it is often impossible in the face of political opposition to translate the findings into policy.

The future significance of evaluation research in the fields of regional planning and urban development will therefore depend on which of these two forces proves the stronger: the pressure of demand, on the one hand, resulting from the problems and tasks involved or the resistance of those who are or who might be affected by the measures concerned as a consequence of their desire to safeguard their advantages on the other. It is quite possible that the capacity of researchers to overcome the present methodological weakness will in the end decide whether the hopes pinned on evaluation research by many people will be fulfilled or whether it will become a theoretical field for individual researchers for whom the translation of findings into policy is only of secondary importance.

NOTES

1. Cf. *Federal Ministry for Regional Planning, Building and Urban Development*, Medium-Term Research Programme "Raumentwicklung und Siedlungsentwicklung" (Regional and Settlement Development); 1974: this programme has since been updated, cf. *Federal Ministry for Regional Planning, Building and Urban Development*, Medium-Term Research Programme "Raumordnung und Stadtebau" (Regional Planning and Urban Development), 1979.
2. Cf. also the interim report covering the period 1974-78 prepared by *P. Runkel*, Das Forschungsprogramm Raum-und Siedlungsentwicklung im Bundesministerium fur Raumordnung, Bauwesen und Stadtebau (The Research Programme "Regional and Settlement Development" of the Federal Ministry for Regional Planning, Building and Urban Development), published in: *Bundesbaublatt* No. 27, 1978, pp. 476 ff.
3. Under Paragraph 4 Section 1 of the Federal Regional Planning Act it is incumbent on the Federal Minister responsible for regional

planning to work towards the realization of the principles of regional planning, in particular by co-ordinating regionally significant planning and measures, including the employment of regionally significant investment.

4. Reasons given for the comparatively late development of evaluation research include "the failure of empirical sociological research to keep pace with developments, the problems which arise when causes are attributed to effects, the inadequate supply of information . . . and the tendency on the part of public "actors" to react rather than to act," cf. *G.M. Hellstern, H. Wollmann,* Arbeitspapier fur den Arbeitskreis "Erfolgskontrolle und Wirkungsanalyse in der Raumordnung" der Akademie fur Raumordnung und Landesplanung (Working paper prepared for the study group "Impact Monitoring and Evaluation Analysis in Regional Planning" of the Academy for regional planning at federal and Land level), December 1978, p. 31.
5. Examples of studies of methods commissioned by the Federal Ministry for Regional Planning, Building and Urban Development include the following: *H. Zimmermann*, Zur Methodik einer Ermittlung der Raumwirksamkeit von Bundesausgaben (Methods of determining the regional significance of federal spending), Marburg, June 1975; a summary of this study may be found in: *Raumforschung und Raumordnung* No. 36, 1978, pp. 95 ff. J. Eekhoff et al., Methoden und Moglichkeiten der Erfolgskontrolle stadtischer Entwicklungsma-Bnahmen (*Methods and Possibilities of Evaluating Urban Development Measures*), Ministry Publications, Brochure No. 03.060. H. Wollmann, G.M. Hellstern, Sanierungsm Banahmen. Stadtebauliche und stadtstrukturelle Wirkungen (Renewal Measures. Impact of Urban Development and Urban Structure Measures: Preliminary Study of Methods). Ministry Publications, Brochure No. 02.012.
6. It is therefore assumed in this paper that it is possible in our society to achieve the consensus necessary for the translation of the findings of evaluation research into policy. This implies that all groups would basically welcome an objective rational decision-making process even if this meant their own interests might be adversely affected. It should be noted that this assumption is not universally accepted.
7. See also the *Federal Government's 1975 Urban Development Report*, pp. 79, and the *Federal Government's 1978 Regional Planning Report*, Bundestag Publication No. 8/2378.
8. For an account of the basic problems involved see *K. Ganser*, Probleme angewandter Forschung (Problems of Applied Research), published in: Information zur Raumentwicklung, 1975, pp. 287 ff.
9. Cf. G.M. Hellstern, H. Wollmann, Zur Leistungsfahigkeit von Fallstudien—am Beispiel einer Sanierungsuntersuchung (An assessment

of the value of case studies using the investigation of arenewal project as an example), published in: P. Kevenhorster, H. Wollmann (eds.), *Kommunalpolitische Praxis und lokale Politikforschung*, Berlin 1978, pp, 349 ff.

10. Similar problems have arisen, for example, in connection with the evaluation of studies commissioned by the Federal Ministry for Regional Planning, Building and Urban Development on the impact of the principal regionally signficant measures taken by the Federation.
11. A statement in support of a greater mixing of methods may be found in G.M. Hellstern, H. Wollmann, Zur Leistungsfahigkeit von Fallstudien, loc. cit., p. 354 and in the other sources mentioned there.
12. This often leads to a situation in which other studies which are relevant but which have been prepared using other methods or have arrived at different results are simply ignored and in the end the discussions of the "right" methods is left to the administration.
13. There is also close co-operation with the research commissioned by the other Ministries of the Federation and the Laender, and with the local authority associations.

THIRTEEN

HELLMUT WOLLMANN

TRENDS IN APPLIED URBAN RESEARCH IN GERMANY*

IN ORDER to give a nutshell report on the development of focus and of subjects of (applied) urban research at German universities, the research activities within the *Urban Research Group* (Arbeitskreis Lokale Politikforschung) in the *German Political Science Association* shall serve as a case in point, also reflecting the comparatively swift changes in focus and orientation that urban research in Germany has undergone within a few years.

URBAN RESEARCH FOCUSSING ON AGGLOMERATION AND ITS ECONOMIC DETERMINANTS

When the Urban Research Group was founded by *Rolf-Richard Grauhan* in 1972, the research work of its members echoed the theoretical and political challenges that social sciences in general were confronted with at the universities in the early 70's in the wake of the student rebellion.

In accordance with the then prevailing *theoretical and conceptual* inclination to put the analysis of politics and administration into the wider framework of "structural" determinants, including particularly the capitalist economy, also many urban researchers concentrated, to begin with, on the processes and effects of agglomeration and deagglomeration

*Paper presented at the European Meeting on Applied Urban Research, 1981.

caused primarily by economic factors and decisions as setting the stage for the "urban process" and as constituting the problem agenda for urban and regional policies[1]. Vis-a-vis an apparent centralization of the decision-making structure both in the economic sector and in the political system, not only in the national but also in the international scale (to mention only the oligopolistic rise of multi-national corporations on the one hand and the growing number of nationally relevant decisions made by international bodies such as the European Community on the other), the (semi-) autonomous status and scope of action of traditional local government was seen to be more and more stripped of substance and, at best, reduced to a legitimizing function.

In the empirical analyses that came out of this phase, special attention was payed to legal rules (such as urban renewal legislation) and institutional arrangements (such as the distribution of public revenues among the federal, state, and local levels of government) through which the "bias of the system"[2] guaranteeing preferential enforcement of the imperatives of the economic system is being translated into and imposed on the local level with, correspondingly, socially discriminatory and selective outcomes.[3]

Inasmuch urban researchers were, in that period, inspired by (Marxist) "class analysis", in their normative orientation they regarded political and social reform as not achievable within the existing capitalist system and power distribution and, hence, viewed reformist strategies as, in the last resort, stabilizing the present system and its ruling elites. Thus, the criteria of "*applied*" urban research could not be siding with and consulting the ruling political and administrative elites, but instead preparing the analytical (and practical) ground for emancipatory processes, valuing the local level as a potential power base for such mobilizing strategies "from the bottom".

Urban Research focussing on intergovernmental relations and implementation processes

In the further course of the 70's, members of the Urban Research Group began empirically to question the alleged centralization tendency particularly in its impact as diminishing and wiping out the scope of action of local government. At the same time, there was a growing interest in the study of decision and implementation processes between and within political agencies and public bureaucracies. This development was largely influenced and fed by a line of research in which the "interrelatedness of policies and political actors" (Politikverflechtung) in the German federal system was analytically tackled[4] and which, in turn, was triggered by the obvious co-ordination and implementation problems into which the Federal Reform programs and legislation ran when facing the administrative momentum and reluctance of Lander and local governments. In a considerable number of empirical studies, members of the Local Research Group investigated, in various policy fields, particularly in spatial, regional and urban planning, the interactions and conflicts which mark the implementation of such policies. Thus, it was shown that the attempts undertaken "from above" to install "centralizing" decision-rules and instruments are often counteracted and thwarted by the actors and agencies "from below" on which implementation of centrally initiated policy depends, demonstrating the strong position which the local level factually has due to this "division of labour" between the layers and levels of government as the "implementing agent".[5]

In terms of their "practice-" orientation, this stage was marked by a growing readiness on the part of urban researchers to accept and support reformist political strategies as a vehicle to bring about social change. Increasingly the communication and cooperation with "practicioners" from cities and towns was sought, not only with members of ("non-elite") citizen-participation and protest groups but also with members of the political and administrative "elites" of local governments.[6]

Urban research as "policy research"

The third stage, since about 1978, has been characterized by a conspicuous sectoral differentation and technical sophistication of urban research. Apparently, this growing *"policy research" and "policy science" orientation* within urban research has been fostered by the fact that a growing number of urban researchers have tapped the "contractual research money market" that, in an expanding volume, is alimented by public agencies, particularly by federal ministries,[7] and in which the evaluation of federal action programs and policy instruments that are highly "legalized" in the German political and administrative culture plays an increasing role, asking particularly for goal-attainment, "implementation deficits" and impacts or "outcomes" at the local level. In obvious response to the new political and administrative demands and to the availability of government funding, urban researchers have also shown a growing interest and readiness to follow and further develop the line of such "policy research", often venturing into detailed and technical analyses of policy instruments (legal provisions, incentive systems, organizational arrangements etc.), and of the course and outcomes of their administrative and bureaucratic implementation. Research of this evaluative sort has been undertaken in an ever wider spectrum of policies, particularly in the fields of urban renewal, housing, environmental, and social policies. The Conference that the Urban Research Group organized on October 1st and 2nd, 1981, concentrating on domestic issues and research, demonstrated the variety of fields and subjects and the "professionalized" technicality that applied urban research has arrived at by now.[8] Furthermore, the considerable number of "practicioners" from all layers of government taking part in that conference documented the degree of cooperation and exchange which has been established between urban researchers at the universities on the one hand and administrators and politicians on the other.[9]

Urban research—towards an integration of basic and applied research ?

As urban research has run the gamut between "structural" and "instrumental" analysis or, to put it differently, between theoretically "critical" basic urban research and empirically "practical" applied urban research, it seems timely and even urgent now to strike a balance as to the assets and liabilities of this development and possibly to reassess and reset its research focus and orientation.

First, it is evident that also in the urban research field the growing number of empirical analyses has not kept abreast of their theoretical potentialities. On the contrary, conceptual reflection and "theory-building" often seem to have been put off or aside amidst the absorption by empirical field research, particularly in the time limitations of urban research of the contractual sort. Yet, theoretical penetration and cumulation are strongly called for, not only in the sake of urban research as *basic* research that is to live up to the traditional disciplinary code of theory-building, but also for maintaining its performance as *applied* urban research that, in order to develop and uphold its explanatory and, consequently, its predictive capabilities, depends very much on the theoretical underpinning that guides and guards its findings and interpretations. Thus, opposing basic and applied (urban) research in a dichotomous way turns out to be detrimental to empirical research undertaken for "practical" purposes.

Second, the more (applied) urban research is wrapped up in the (legal, technical and other) details and the mere "instrumentality" of policies, the more it tends to be analytically stuck with the concrete contingency of that "instrumentality" and to neglect the historical, economic, societal etc. setting which may preclude or admit instrumental alternatives. To maintain a "critical distance" to the very concreteness of its objects is not only vital for basic research in order to keep its "search for truth" aloof from the partisan interests in the field to be analyzed, but is, again, also essential for applied research in order to enable i to "think ahead" and to bring in "social imagination" where the political and administrative practice of the day may still be unattentive or blind to alternative courses of action.

As to relevant substantive problems on the agenda of an urban research that should integrate basic and applied research in order to be both theoretically and practically relevant, reconsidering and possibly redrafting the societal and political functions of local government and the local level is particularly called for. As, on the one hand, the "etatistic" fabric and thrust of the modern welfare state with its overregulating and bureaucratizing tendencies appear to become, in essential parts, ineffective, if not counterproductive and, on the other hand, letting the "market forces" prevail seems to be, in many areas, hardly acceptable because of the "social blindness" and distributional failures of the market, local government and the local level are likely to gain an increasing societal and political function, not as a subterfuge of fiscal crisis management and a "scapegoat" of central-state policy failures, but as an arena and domain of locally determined and performed processes of problem solving and service delivery that may avoid the "bureaucratic costs" of central-state intervention without forfeiting substantial accomplishments and standards of the modern social state. In order to tap the experiences made and research undertaken in other countries, German urban research will have to intensify the exchange with the international research and to step up its own comparative research efforts. The Urban Research Group that has been largely restricted to domestic problems and research so far is presently setting such steps.

Steps in German (applied) urban research in general

This sketch is explicitly limited to some developmental lines in regard to the Urban Research Group. Other contributors and contributions to the development of urban research can be mentioned here only briefly, the brevity being solely imposed by the page limitations of this statement and not in the least meant to belittle the bearing of these other contributions.

Mention should be made of the *Section of Regional and Urban Sociology* ("Sektion Stadt- und Regionalsoziologie") (within the German Sociological Association), members of which have undertaken remarkable steps in the university context towards pursuing cross-national comparative research.[10]

Founded in 1973 as a center for applied urban research, funded by West-German cities and towns and meant to do "consulting" research for the member cities, "*Deutsches Institute fur Urbanistik*" (German Urban Institute) in Berlin has established its reputation as a nucleus of applied urban research outside the universities.[11]

Whereas contractual research funded by public agencies, particularly by federal and state ministries, promoted, as mentioned, albeit indirectly and in an adhoc fashion, a broadening flux of applied urban research, general research funding by the pertinent institutions and foundations has only slowly responded to the growing societal need for urban research. "*Deutsche Forschungsgemeinschaft*" (German Science Foundation) discussed the formation of a research focus (Forschungsschwerpunkt) on urban and regional research for some years without materializing it, after all.[12] It was the *Robert Bosch Foundation* that decided in 1977 to inaugurate an Urban Research Program concentrating on the intra-regional mobility of households and enterprises and on (federal, state, regional, and local) policies to influence it, picking the Region of Greater Stuttgart as a "target area" of research and setting up a five years' time horizon (1977/1982).[13] The program is explicitly designed as "*applied basic urban research*" in the sense that, on the one hand, it aims at theory-building particularly by means of "longitudinal" research methods permitted by the five years' research period, and, on the other hand, "testing" and diffusion of research results in continuous "feedback loops" with practicioners in the field are expected to be performed by the research teams particularly towards the end of the research program proper.

Presently, the *Volkswagen Foundation* is engaged in considerations and deliberations about setting up a new research focus on urban research that would probably also comprise cross-national comparative research. A decision has not been reached as yet.

REFERENCES

1. See Rolf-Richard Grauhan. Elifuhrung: Lokale Politikforschung, in: Rolf-Richard Grauhan (ed.), *Lokale Politikforschung*, Vol. 1, Frankfurt/New York (Campus Verlag) 1975, p. 11 ff.; *Adalbert Evers*, Agglomerationsprozeß und Stadtsfunktionen, in: ibid., p. 41 ff.
2. For the concept of "selectivity rules" ("Selektivitatsregeln") that *Claus Offe* developped, partly drawing on E.E. Schattschneider's concept of the "bias of the system" and on the concept of "non-decisions" formulated by P. Bachrach and S. Baratz, see *Claus Offe*, Klassenherrschaft und politisches System, Die Selektivitat politischer

Institutionen, in: Claus Offe, Strukturprobleme des Kapitalistischen Staates, Frankfurt (edition suhrkamp), 1972, p. 65 ff.

3. For a collection of papers of the first period of the Urban Research Group (1972-1974) see Rolf-Richard Grauhan (ed.). *Lokale Politikforschung*, 2 volumes, Frankfurt/New York (Campus Verlag), 1975.
4. See Fritz W. Scharpf; Bernd Reissert; Fritz Schnabel, *Politikverflechtung*, Konlgstein (Athenaum-Verlag), 1976.
5. For a collection of papers out of this second period (1974-1978) see Hellmut Wollmann (ed.), *Politik im Dickicht der Burokratie*, Beitrage Zur Implementationsforschung, Sonderband 3/1979, Leviathan, Opladen (Westdeutscher Verlag) 1980. For a project report out of this context see Angelika Baestlein et al., State Grants and Local Development Planning in the Federal Republic of Germany, in: *Kenneth Hanf, Fritz W. Scharpf* (eds.), *Interorganizational Policy Making, Limits to Coordination and Central Control*, London, Beverly Hills (Sage Publication), 1978, p. 115 ff.
6. For conceptual papers particularly considering the interaction between research and practice, see the papers delivered in the meeting of urban researchers within the 1977 Conference of the German Political Science Association, published in Paul Kevenhorster, Hellmut Wollmann (eds.), *Kommunalpolitische Praxis und lokale Politikforschung*, Berlin (Deutsches Institut fur Urbanistik, Eigenverlag), 1978.
7. Referring to this development, see the statement by Dr. Hans Pflaumer from the Federal Ministry for Housing and Urban Development in this volume. For a more detailed discussion of the development of evaluation research in Germany see Gerd-Michael Hellstern, Hellmut Wollmann, The Contribution of Evaluation to Administration, in: Robert A. Levine, Marian A. Solomon, Gerd-Michael Hellstern, Hellmut Wollman (eds.), *Evaluation Research and Practice, Comparative and International Perspectives*, Beverly Hills, London (Sage Publication), 1981, p. 67 ff.
8. For a selection of papers to this conference see Jens Joachim Hesse, Hellmut Wollmann (eds.), *Lokale Politikforschung*, Frankfurt (Campus-Verlag) 1982. For the results of some of the working subgroups within this conference see Jochen Hucke, Reinhard Ueberhorst (eds.), *Kommunale Umweltpolitik*, Basel (Birkhauser-Verlag) 1982; Dieter Schimanke Hans Haverkamph (eds.), Kommunal Entercklungspolitik, Basel (Birkaauser verlage) 1982; Peter Grottian, Wilfried Nelles (eds.), *Groβstadt und soziale Bewegungen*, Basel (Birkhauser-Verlag) 1982; Adalbert Evers, Hellmut Wollmann (eds.), *Kommunale Wohnungspolitik*, Basel (Birkhauser-Verlag) 1982.
9. For another recent conference that was organized by Deutscher Stadtetag and "Hochschule fur Verwaltungswissenschaft Speyer" in October 1981 and which dealt with improving the exchange between

universities and cities, between "gown and town", see Zusammenarbeit Stadt/Hochschule (Neue Schriften des Deutschen Stadtetages), Koln (Kohlhammer-Verlag), 1982.

10. See the reports by Prof. Jurgen Friedrichs, Hamburg, and Prof. Bernd Hamm, Trier, in this volume.
11. See the report by Dr. Werner Heinz in this volume.
12. Thomas Sieverts, Hochschulforschung auf dem Gebiet der Stadt-und Regionalplanung, in: *Bundesforschungsanstalt fur Landeskunde und Raumordnung* (ed.), Wer forscht was fur die raumliche Planung?-Sachstand und Perspektiven–, Bonn 1978, p. 222 f.
13. For first results of the research program in which four (partly universitarian, partly commercial) research teams are engaged, see Robert Bosch Stiftung (ed.), *Beitrage Zur Stadtforschung*, vol. 1, Stuttgart (Dt. Verlagsanstalt) 1979, and vol. 2, Stuttgart (Dt. Verlagsanstalt) 1982.

FOURTEEN

JACQUES PERNELLE

URBAN RESEARCH IN FRANCE*

SOME BASIC DATA ON THE DEVELOPMENT OF URBAN RESEARCH

SINCE the 1920's university researchers in France have devoted part of their research activities on urban phenomena: Particularly the geographers analysed the transition of France from a so far predominantly rural to an urbanized society. But it was the accelerated pace of urbanization in the 60's that triggered the interest of government agencies: the construction of traffic infrastructure, the management of land, the development of housing, particularly of social housing and policies meant to regulate urban growth caused a conspicuous increase of research efforts.

Particularly the 5th and 6th Plan for Economic and Social Development lead to the employment of research that was commissioned by administrative agencies to mobilize all pertinent fields of research: engineering, building, economics and social sciences.

From 1965 to 1975, the expenditure of considerable public research funds resulted in activating a growing number of researchers on subjects that were quite often closely related to preparing and critically evaluating public policies.

Today, research is confronted with reduced growth and is at the eve of a profound reorientation. It has to adapt itself to a

*Paper presented at the European Meeting on Applied Urban Research, 1981.

new situation characterized by the decentralization of the decision processes, by changes in the labour market and by value changes in life styles.

INSTITUTIONS

Distinctions should be made between

1. the agencies for programming and financing research,
2. the performance of research and the organization of researchers,
3. the diffusion of research.

The agencies for programming research

a. *Le Ministere de l'Urbanisme et du Logement* ("Ministry of Urbanism and Housing"), with three units:

—*La Mission de la Recherche Urbaine* ("Commission of Urban Research"), focal point of the network ONU/CEE,

—*Le Plan Construction* ("Planning and Construction"), an interministerial body *mainly engaged in Construction and Housing*,

—*Le Service de la Recherche Architecturale* ("Service of Architectural Research").

—*Le Centre de Documentation d'Urbanisme* ("Center for Documentation of Urbanism").

b. *Le Ministere du Plan et de l'Amenagement du territoire* ("Ministry of Planning and Spatial Planning"), which particulary initiated research on regional economy and planning,

c. *Le Ministere des Transports* ("Ministry of Transport"), particularly for the section Urban Transport ("*Transports urbains*"),

d. *Le Ministere de l'Environnement* ("Ministry of the Environment"), on questions of urban ecology,

e. *Le Ministere de la Recherche et de la Technologie*

("Ministry of Research and Technology"), coordinating the entire research in France.

The agencies for conducting research

To a good part, research is carried out by a number of private research institutions, but above all in the following units:

a. *Le Centre National de la Recherche Scientifique* ("National Center of Scientific Research"), in research laboratories that are divided up by the major research disciplines,
b. the universities with a considerable statutory autonomy since 1968,
c. *Les Unites Pedagogiques d'Architecture* ("Pedagogic Units of Architecture") (25),
d. *Le Centre Scientifique et Technique du Batiment* ("Scientific and Technical Center of Building"),
e. *Le Laboratoire Central Ides Ponts et Chaussees* ("Central Laboratory of Bridge and Road Construction"),
f. *L'Insttiut de Recherche sur les Transports* ("Research Institute on Transport").

As the research topics in this field are predominantly interdisciplinary, it was necessary to maintain a strong administrative coordination of the projects.

Also the close connection with agrarian research should be stressed. Thus, research can also be considered as carried out particularly by the following public research agencies:

(i) *L'Institut d'Amenagement et d'Urbanisme de la Region Ile de France* ("Institute for Spatial Planning and Urbanism of the Region Ile de France"),
(ii) *Les Etablissements publics des villes nouvelles*,
(iii) the institutions for research concerning public transport,
(iv) the agencies for urbanism in greater agglomerations,
(v) the centers for professional technical studies (HLM, Building . .).

DISSEMINATION AND THE PROVISION OF ACCESS TO RESEARCH

Material of documentation and information is available in each of the administrative centers mentioned above but the main documentation centers are:

(i)	*Le C.S.T.B.* (as to materials, systems, standards),	4, Avenue du Recteur Poincare *75016 Paris*
(ii)	*Le Plan Construction* (informaation service concerning the policies of housing and technology),	1, rue Francois ler *75008 Paris*
(iii)	*Le Centre de Documentation d'Urbanisme* ("Documentation Center of Urbanism") (Databank publishing the Analytical Papers of Urban Research in English, Spanish and French),	64, run de la Federation *75015 Paris*
(iv)	*Le Centre documentaire des Sciences Humaines* ("Documentation Center of Human-Sciences")	MSH 54, Boulevard Raspail *75007 Paris*
(v)	*L'Institut Francais d'Architecture* ("French Institute of Architecture"),	6, rue de Tournon *75006 Paris*
(vi)	*La Delegation a l'Amenagement du Territoire et a l'Action Regionale*, DATAR ("Commission of Spatial Planning and Regional Management").	1, avenue Charles Floquet *75007 Paris*

Publications

As outlet for French urban research should be mentioned:

La revue 'U' et les fiches analytiques annuelles (CDU),

Les collections du Plan Construction,

Les cahiers du CSTB,

Les annales de la recherche urbaine,
Les bulletins signaletiques du CDSH,
Metropolis,
Espaces et societes.

FIFTEEN

ERWIN ZIMMERMANN

URBAN COMMUNITY RESEARCH IN SWITZERLAND
Past and Future*

URBAN RESEARCH IN SWITZERLAND

URBAN studies in Switzerland may be related to three major research traditions: *Urbanization-Migration process and urban ecology*, *Local autonomy and federalism*, *Community power and decision-making*. This brief overview only intends to provide some guidance to the relevant literature and does not attempt a systematic substantive review.

Urbanization and Migration processes and their social, economic and political consequences have received growing attention in the 1970s. Rossi's recent book *Sviluppo urbano e politica urbana in Svizzera* (1979) contains well informed and authoritative statements on urban processes and policies in Switzerland. *Modernization without urbanization* by Gardner Clark (1979) puts the Swiss urban phenomenon in a internationally comparative perspective. By international standards Swiss urbanization has been very slow and basically related to the growing importance of services industries after Second World War. Bassand and Brulhardt (1980) make the point on a large number of theoretical and empirical studies related to migration and spatial mobility. Current policy oriented research questions the functionality of the Swiss urban system (Guller et

*Paper presented at the European Meeting on Applied Urban Research, 1981.

al. 1980a) in the context of deepening economic status differentials among Swiss regions.[1] The *urban ecology* approach has been predominant in several recent studies of major urban agglomerations (Hamm 1977 and 1980: Guller *et al.* 1980b; Muggli 1980). Following the Chicago School tradition various aspects of urban living and local political participation have been analyzed (Vontobel 1976; Campiche and Zimmermann 1973-75; Neidhart and Hoby 1977).

In the traditional *institutional approach to local autonomy* (Jagmetti 1972), the autonomy of municipalities is defined as the capacity to accomplish under conditions of independence certain public tasks within the limits of the Constitution and the laws (Meylen et al. 1972, p. 33). However legally defined communal autonomy varies to a great deal from Canton to Canton. After careful examination of the Federal and Cantonal constitutional laws Meylan (1972) reaches the following general conclusion: Local *autonomy* of municipalities is very high with regards to local territorial planning, law and order, the use of public property, the public regulation of commerce, schools (especially in terms of the selection of teachers) and the hiring of personal staffing the local administration. In fiscal matters local autonomy is more limited: the fiscal system and the tax rates are largely imposed by the Cantons, but the fixation of the taxing coefficient can be quite freely handled by municipalities. Concerning public health and public assistance, fire and civil protection, local autonomy is very weak. In an interesting exploratory study, Geser (1977) has analyzed empirically the variation among Cantons with regard to their definition of municipal competence and duties. Results tend to show that legally defined autonomy is weakest in economically highly developed and urbanized Cantons. This is to suggest a higher degree of *centralization.* Rene L. Frey *Zwischen Foderalismus und Zentralismus* (1977) has made a very significant contribution to the federalism discussion in Switzerland from the point of view of the economic theory of federalism. Costs of public goods accruing to society at large are related to the "federalism-centralism" dimension in a U-shaped curve, where the minimum characterizes the optimal degree of centralization. As a result of such considerations, the economic theory of federalism allows predictions about the kinds of tasks best performed at the different levels of government. Frey's work includes specific propositions about the "optimal" division of public tasks and fiscal arrangements between the Confederation and the Cantons. However, only marginal attention is given to the role of municipalities in the federal State. Swiss municipalities contribute about one fourth of the total national tax income and participate at the rate of 28 per cent in total public expenditures. Moreover, municipalities are responsible for the implementation of various policies designed at the two higher levels of government.

Research on *community power and decision-making structures* has been initiated by Michel Bassand in the late 1960s inspired by early American community studies (Bassand, 1974, and Bassand and Fragniere, 1976/1978). A very lucid study of community conflict over political power is provided by Windisch (1976). Sociologist have by no means been the only ones to study community politics. Law professionals, political scientists, economists, geographers have contributed a lot to the understanding of political community autonomy, community typology, local administration, citizen participation and so forth. It is not necessary to review these works here as excellent review articles have recently become available (Linder, 1980 and Bassand, 1980).[2] Despite the existence of quite a few community studies in Switzerland regarding particular aspects of decision-making or policy outputs and implementation, we know very little about the most significant patterns of variation in "community politics" among Swiss political municipalities. We know even less, if and how such patterns affect policy performance and implementation. Large-n comparative urban research has been scarce in Switzerland. There are, however, two important exceptions: Bassand (1974) established a typology of urban communities in Switzerland on the basis of 162 municipalities which had in 1960 a population of 5.000 and more. In his study, Pommerehne (1977) has used a median voter model for explaining public expenditure patterns in the 111 largest Swiss municipalities.

Major urban data sources and files in Switzerland

In 1970, Switzerland counted 3072 politically autonomous municipalities from which 377 may be regarded as urban places. Municipalities are also called "communes" or "Gemeinden." A municipality has city status if its population amounts to 10.000 or more residents. Urban agglomerations are defined on the basis of mobility flows from residence to work. About 58 per cent of the Swiss population (6.270.000 in 1970) live in these 377 urban communities. The brief and incomplete overview of urban data sources to be presented here is based on information I was able to obtain through my professional networks. A systematic effort is currently under way, sponsored by the Swiss Political Science Association.[3]

There are only few official institutions in Switzerland which collect comparable data for all urban municipalities. Nevertheless, the data remain dispersed and there is nothing like the *US City and County Data Book* made available in print and machine readable from. The inexistence of a comprehensive inventory of urban data from such institutions such as the Census makes the task of a comprehensive overview even more difficult.[4] However, several efforts of documenting and archiving urban data have been undertaken or are currently plnnned.

The *Swiss Census* provides by far the most data through the *Census of Population* (1950, 60, 70, 80, etc.) and the Census of *Employment and Industry* (1965, 75, etc.). Census data are indeed collected for all the 3072 Swiss municipalities and published about 2-3 years latter. These results are also available on computer types in "table form" and not on an "all variables by case" base. More selectively reported census data for cities can also be found in the Swiss Statistical Yearbook edited by the Federal Bureau for Statistics. Data on *Public Finances* are collected by the *Federal Finance Administration.*[5] They are published every year for the 25 largest Swiss cities. Data on all Swiss municipalities may be obtained on request in computer readable form. Data on local government revenues and expenditures exist in considerable detail. Two other public institutions provide selective data for the 92 Swiss cities.

The *Federal Bureau for Industry, Commerce and Work*[6] collects various kinds of economic data for private and government demands. The data are periodically published in the "La vie economique—Rapports economiques et de statistique sociale" by the Department of Political Economy. The *Association of Swiss Cities*[7] has 119 members but not all of the 92 cities with more than 10.000 population are among these members. Selective official and special purpose statistics are published yearly in the Annuaire statistique des Villes Suisses.

Several research institutions have set up *urban community data files* for specific purposes over the last 10 years or so. However, many of these data archiving efforts remain unknown and many data sets are insufficiently documented. We are aware of only *three* major efforts in this area:

(1) *The Information-Raster* by the Federal Bureau for Statistics.[8] The information raster file is available in raw data form on type. It contains about 500 census variables (1950-1975) for all the 3072 Swiss municipalities. The codebook is available on request and at no cost. The data file, however, is not free and costs depend on the data quantity, but also on computer time used to satisfy the special wishes of a particular client.

(2) *The 3072 Swiss Municipalities file* by the Department of Sociology at the University of Zurich. The data set is constituted as a SPSS file with several hundred variables for all 3072 municipalities. Besides census data, the file includes some indications regarding the local political systems and referenda voting[9].

(3) *The 111 Largest Cities File* by the Institute for Empirical Research in Economics at the University of Zurich. The data file contains about 400 variables for the 111 largest cities in 1970. The variables pertain to selective demographic and socioeconomic community characteristics, but also to voting and fiscal policy.[10]

CONCLUSIONS

Swiss urban research efforts in the past have been characterized by several limitations and future prospects are not too good. Recent fiscal and social problems in several Swiss cities, have however, created a more favorable national political climate for urban research. As a consequence, the Swiss National Science

Foundation plans to set up a special emphasis program on urban problems within the next two years or so. Funding for such a program could indoubtedly provide considerable stimulation for researchers to put together their specific resources and eventually to participate in international comparative efforts. Without such a program, urban research in Switzerland might well remain an area of occasional studies carried out with very limited financial resources for many years to come.

NOTES

1. A special NSF program on "Regional Problems" has been initiated since 1978. The program is directed by Mr. Brugger, E.A., Bundesgasses 8, CH-3003 Bern.
2. For the best available review of research on "community politics" in Switzerland see "Politique local en Suisse—Kommunalpolitik in der Schweiz", in *Annuaire suisse de science politique*, vol 20 (Raimund E. Germann ed.), Bern: Editions Paul Haupt, 1980, p. 285.
3. Mr. Euben Horber of the Political Science Department at the University of Geneva has sent a comprehensive questionnaire to a large number of private and public research institutions in Switzerland about urban research and data collection activities (Universite de Geneva, 2, rue Condolle, CH-1200 Geneva 4).
4. Mr. Peter Schutz of the Swiss Federal Bureau Statistics (information service) is the well known living memory. It is good to get in touch with him when all other guides to official data have failed to provide the wanted information on Swiss statistics (Hallwystrasse 15, CH-300 Bern).
5. Administration federale des finances—Eidgenossiche Finanzverwaltung)Bernerhof, CH-3000 Bern).
6. Office federal de l'industrie, des arts et metiers et du travail (OFIAMT) Bundesmat fur Industrie, Gewerbe und Arbeit (BIGA, Bundesgasse 8, CH-3003 Bern).
7. Union des villes suisses—Schweizerischer Stadtverband, Junkerngasse 56, 3011 Bern.
8. In french, the "Information raster" is called "grille d'information". The person to get in touch with is Mr. Claude Grandjean from the Federal Bureau of Statistics.
9. For further information write to Professor Peter Heintz, University of Zurich, *Wiesenstrasse* 9, CH-8008 Zurich.
10. Write to Professor W. Pommerehne, Institute for Empirical Research in Economics, Forchstrasse 145, CH-8032 Zurich.

REFERENCES

Bassand, M. Problems at tendances de la recherche sur la politique local. In: *Annuaire suisse de science politique*. Vol. 20. Paul Haupt, 1980, pp. 39-61.

Bassand, M. *Urbanisation et pouvoir politique: Le cas de la Suisse*. Geneva: Ed. Georg, 1974.

Bassand, M., et Brulhardt. *Mobilite spatial*. St-Saphorin, Lavaux-CH: Georgi, 1980.

Bassand, M., et Frangiere J.P., *Le pouvoir dans la ville*. Vevey: Ed. Delta, 1978.

Campiche, R.J. and Zimmermann, E., *Changement social et communaute*. 9 volumes. Lausanne, Switzerland: Institut d'Ethique sociale, 1973-1975.

Clark, Gardner, Modernization without Urbanization or Switzerland as a Model of Job Development Outside Urban Areas, In *Revue Suisse de Sociologie*. 6, 1979 pp. 1-42.

Fischer, G., *Der Wohlstand der Kantone*, Bern, Paul Haupt, 1980.

Frey, R.L., Ein volkswirtschaftliches Konzept des schweizerischen Bundesstaates. *Zwischen foderalismus und Zentralismus* Bern und Frankfurt, 1977.

Germann, R.E. (ed.), Politique local en Suisse—Kommunalpolitik in der Schweiz. In *Annuaire Suisse de Science Politique*, 1980.

Geser, H., Kantonale Gemeindeorganisation im rechtssoziologischen Vergleich Eine Inhaltanalyse von Gesetzestexten. In *Schweizerische Zeitschrift fur Soziologie*. Nr. 2/77, 1977, pp. 111-141.

Guller, P. et al., Funktionalitat des schweizerischen Stadtsystems—Ein Versuch zur Einbezug der Stadte in die Raumordnungspolitik. *Nationales Forschungs-Programm Regionalprobleme*, 1980b, p. 103.

Guller, P. et al., Entflechtungs—und Vermischungsprozesse in urbanen Raumen—Empirische Untersuchungen in den Agglomerationen Zurich, Basel und Lugano. *Arbeitsberichte Nr. 12, Nationales Forschungsprogramm*. Regionalprobleme in der Schweiz, 1980b, p. 371.

Hamm, B., Stadtentwicklung, Stadtstruktur und Wohnstandortwahl. In *Schriftenreiche Wohnungswesen*. Bern, Ch: Bundesamt fur Wohnungswesen, 1980.

Hamm, B., *Die Organisation der stadtischen Umwelt*. Frauenfeld/Stuttgart, 1977.

Jagmetti, R., Die Stellung der Gemeinden. *Zeitschrift fur Schweizerisches Recht*. Band 91, pp. 221-400, 1972.

Linder, W., Zur Einfuhrung: Kommunalpolitik im Spiegel Schweizerischer und Deutscher Literatur. In *Annuaire suisse de science politique*. Vol. 20. (ed. R.E. Germann), Bern, Switzerland: Editions Paul Haupt, pp. 9-37, 1980.

Meylan, J., Problemes actuals de l'autonomie communale. In *Zeitschrift fur Schweizerisches Recht*. Band 91, pp. 1-225, 1972.

Meylan, J., Gottraux, M., Dahinden, P., *Schweizerische Gemeinden und Gemeinde—Autonomie*, Lausanne, 1972.

Neidhart, L. and Hoby, J., *Ursachen der gegenwartigen Stimmabstinenz in der Schweiz*. Zurich, 1977.

Pommerehne, W.W., Institutional Approaches to Public Expenditures: Empirical Evidence from Swiss Municipalities. *Institute for Empirical Research in Economics Paper*. Nr. 7708, 1977.

Rossi, A., *Sviluppo urbano et politica urbana in Svizzera*. Lugano Edizioni Trelingue, 1979.

Rossi, A. and Tami, P., Development urbain en Suisse et politique urbaine de la Confederation. *DISP*. Nr. 52, January 1979, pp. 16-22 and *DISP*. Nr. 53, August 1979, pp. 15-22 1979.

Vontobel, J., *Zum Bischpiel X-Wil, eine Gemeindestudie, Menschlige Umwelt im Wandel*, Zurich, 1976.

Windisch, U., *Lutte de Clans—Lutte de Classes*, Lausanne, 1976.

SIXTEEN

HENK VOOGD

URBAN RESEARCH IN THE NETHERLANDS*

INTRODUCTION

IN THIS note an overview is given of some major urban issues in the Netherlands. Besides, some information will be presented about research institutes and agencies who are involved in urban research. To avoid misunderstanding, this note does not claim to be complete.

Some major issues

The tone for recent investigations in the field of urban research was set by the "Urbanization Report" of the Dutch National Government of 1976. The two key issues of the report are the functioning of the urban centres and the control of urban growth. In order to combat the decline of the bigger cities and to prevent undesired urban sprawl a policy was proposed directed to reinforcement of urban activities. It is aimed at balanced commuting conditions for urban agglomerations, which implies a reduced growth of mobility associated with job commuting. This necessitates an increase of the residential attractiveness of the various cities. Recent urban research activities therefore strongly focus on urban revitalization and renovation.

*Paper presented at the European Meeting on Applied Urban Research, 1981.

Much research is concentrated on the urban agglomerations in the western part of the country. An important problem concerns the foreign immigration. In the period of 1975-1979 one had to cope with a migration surplus of over 65.000 people. This figures grows in importance by taking into consideration that the large majority of the foreign migrants went to live in the large urban agglomerations in the already crowded western part of the country, such as Amsterdam and Rotterdam. Recently, some research has been finished in which the consequences of integration policies with respect to foreign inhabitants of cities have been investigated (Erasmus University).

Review articles and publications

1. *Current Trends and Policies in Housing and Building in 1978*, The Hague (Ministry of Housing and Planning), (1979).
2. Faludi, A., *Promotion and Control of Development in The Netherlands*, University of Amsterdam, Institute for Planning and Demography, 1978.
3. *Housing in The Netherlands, Facts and Figures*, The Hague, Ministry of Housing and Physical Planning, 1979.
4 Nijkamp, P., Urbanization Policy: Plans and Possibilities, *Planning and Development in The Netherlands*, IX, 2, 1977, 115-134.
5. *Summary of the Report on Urbanization in The Netherlands*, The Hague, Ministry of Housing and Physical Planning, 1976.
6. *Urban and Regional Research in The Netherlands; an annotated list*, The Hague, Ministry of Housing and Physical Planning (undated).
7. Voogd, H., Issues and Tendencies in Dutch Regional Planning. In: Hudson, R. & J. Lewis (eds), *Regional Planning in Europe*, Pion, London, 1982.
8. Witsen, J., Some general aspects of the Urbanization Report of The Netherlands, *Planning and Administration*, 2, 1977, 76-85.

Major Research Institutes (a short list)

1. Ministerie van Volkshuisvesting en Ruimtelijke Ordening, P.O. Box 20951, 2500 EZ Den Haag (Housing Issues)
2. Ministerie van Volkshuisvesting en Ruimtelijke Ordening, P.O. Box 3001, 2700 KA Zoetermeer (Urban renewal).
3. Rijksplanologische Dienst, P.O. Box 90618, 2596 BK Den Hagg (Urban and Regional Planning).
4. Research Centre for Physical Planning TNO (PSC-TNO), P.O. Box 45, 2600 AA Delft (urban development, mathematical modelling).
5. Netherlands Economic Institute, Burgemeester Oudlaan 50, 2000 DR Rotterdam (urban development, mathematical modelling).
6. Stichting Bouwcentrum, Weena 700, 3014 DA Rotterdam (housing).
7. Vereniging van Nederlandse Gemeenten, Nassaulaan 12, 2514 JS Den Haag (Representative of all Dutch Municipalities).

SEVENTEEN

ZDRAVKO MLINAR

URBAN SOCIAL RESEARCH IN YUGOSLAVIA*

YUGOSLAVIA is a country with a relatively very low level but at the same time with a high rate of urbanization. There are three characteristic approaches to the urban social research in Yugoslavia: The first may be exemplified by the literature which represent (urban-rural) sociology and political science as a new fields of university education. Here we find several textbooks, manuals and general discussions on cities, on process of urbanization, industrialization, on conceptual and theoretical issues concerning the spatio-structural and developmental dimensions of cities, the questions concerning a marxist approach and ideological issues of the urban question etc. Some attention was paid also to the alternative disciplinary conceptualizations of this field like: urban sociology, sociology of the local communities, sociology of settlements, local ("communal") politics and others (C. Kostic 1974, Z. Mlinar 1973, S. Suvar 1973, V. Lay 1975, V. Simovic 1966).

Research in several neighbouring disciplines—which have a longer tradition than sociology and political science—has to be considered as well; especially in demography, social geography, ethnology and history (D. Vogelnik 1961, I. Ginic 1967, I. Vriser 1972).

Second broader issue area concerns local politics and especially

*Paper presented at the European Meeting on Applied Urban Research, 1981.

the wide complexity of self-management within urban context and in the process of urbanization. These studies and research projects can be distinguished into two categories: (a) there is a smaller number of studies which are primarily focusing on urban politics (S. Tomic 1972, S. Bakic—in: M. Zivkovic 1977); (b) a wider range of studies primarily dealing with the political process (self-management) as such, but specifying the differences between urban and rural areas or indicating the characteristics of the urban context (E. Pusic 1968, R. Marinkovic 1971, P. Jambrek 1975, A Barbic—K. Boh 1969).

The process of decentralization and of withering away of state coercive intervention represented a challenge for (urban) social research. The new political system, especially its normative-programatic and institutional dimension, exposed the need for more research on the actual behaviour of citizens in urban and rural communities and of actual functioning of the new institutional structure of (local) self-government. The focus of research was especially the actual political and social participation of the inhabitants, the (re-) distribution of influence, the process of reconciliation of different interests, local-national linkages, centre-periphery relations etc. (E. Pusic 1981, D. Mircev 1976, F. Bucar—J. Smidovnik 1975, P. Jacob 1971, F. Vreg 1978).

The concern for processes which either strengthen or hinder the formation of a socialist community and humanization of everyday life was considered in studies of local (neighborhood) communities or at the level of commune-encompasing a town and its catchment area (C. Ribicic 1979).

The third characteristic approach to urban research indicates—the most frequent-studies which represent a response to the concrete, practical needs of urban and spatial planning. This includes the analysis of the planning process itself (the actors, planning goals and objectives . . .) as well as the spatial organization of cities as an instrument which is manipulable and can be used to promote basic social values (M. Zivkovic 1971, Z. Mlinar, P. Gantar, D. Kos 1981, D. Seferagic, V. Lay, O. Caldarovic, 1981, S. Vujovic 1974).

In this sense there is a question of the optimal size of the (neighborhood) community and of the city, of the relationship between work—place and the housing environment, of the role of community centre, of the interrelationship of physical (settlement) structure and social structure, density of settlement, the type of buildings etc. (S. Vujovic, V. Macura 1971, R. Jakhel 1979, Z. Mlinar—B. Kavcic 1965, M. Zivkovic 1981, L. Sarec—A. Gulic 1981).

Other "classic" issues of urban social research are considered as well like e.g.: housing preferences and housing estates (J. Makarovic 1980, S. Bjelajac—in L. Sarec 1977, M. Zivkovic 1975), rural-urban migrations (D. Vogelnik, A Ferligoj, S. Splichal 1980), tendencies toward suburbanization (D. Seferagic 1975), problems of commuting, leisure-time activities, patterns of interpersonal relations between neighbours, friendship and kinship relationships in cities and new housing estates (M. Ahtik—in: M. Zivkovic 1977) spatial distribution of criminal acts and youth delinquency in cities (J. Pecar 1975, A. Todorovic 1971).

Urban researchers are acting within universities (e.g. in Zagreb, Ljubljana, Beograd, Sarajevo) town planning offices and in other institutions. They are organized within Yugoslav Sociological Association. Several national and international symposia were organized like e.g.: on industrialization and urbanization processes in Yugoslavia (Dubrovink, 1971); "Comparative Ecological Analysis of Social Change" (in cooperation with ISA—Ljubljana 1976), "Urban Housing Environment" (L. Sarec 1977), "Polish-Yugoslav Seminar" on urban social structure and development (Ljubljana, 1980).

Federal Statistical Office provides census and other data on settlements (more limited), local communities and communes (wider range), some of them are available as time series. Standing Conference of Towns and Communes of Yugoslavia is dealing with the current issues of urban development and publishing a monthly review "Komuna".

REFERENCES

Barbic, Ana, Katja Boh: Politicna participacija obcana v krajevni skupnosti (*Political participation of citizen in the local community*), Institut za sociologijo in filozofijo, Ljubljana, 1969.

Bucar, F., Smidovnik, J., *Javna uprava in obcan*, FSPN, Ljubljana, 1975.

Jambrek, Peter, *Development and Social Change in Yugoslavia*, Lexington: Saxon House, 1975

Jakhel, Rudi Iluzija in resnicnost urbanih sredisc (*Ilusion and reality of urban centers*), Cankarjeva zalozba, Ljubljana 1979.

Jacob, Philip et. al., *Values and the Active Community*, Free Press, New York, 1971.

Kostic, Cvetko, Sociologija grada (*Urban Sociology*), Izdavacko-informativni centar studenata, Beograd 1974.

Lay, Vladimir, Razvoj urbane sociologije u Hrvatskoj (*Development of urban* sociology in Croatia), *Revija za sociologiju*, Vol. 5. No. 4, Zegreb 1975.

Makarovic, Jan, Problemi stanovanjske izgradnje v luci vrednot samoupravne druzbe (Problems of housing construction in the light of the values of self-management society), FSPN, Ljubljana 1980.

Marinkovic, Radivoje, Ko odlucje u komuni (Who makes decisions in the commune), Institut drustvenin nauka, Beograd 1971.

Mircev, Dimitar, The New Yugoslav Commune: A structure for development, SOECO Papers, FSPN, Ljubljana, 1976.

Mlinar, Zdravko, Sociologija lokalnih skupnost (Sociology of local communities), FSPN, Ljubljana, 1974.

Mlinar, Zdravko, Kavcic, Bogdan et al., Ljudje v novem mestu (People the new town), Velenje 1965, Institut za sociologijo in filozofijo, Ljubljana, 1965.

Mlinar, Zdravko, Teune, Henry, (edit), *Social Ecology of Change: From Equilibrium to Development*, Sage Publications, London 1978.

Mlinar, Zdravko, Pavel Gantar, Drago Kos, Prostorska organizacija in razvojne teznje v mestu Nova Gorica (Spatial organization and development tendencies in the town Nova Gorica), FSPN, Ljubljana, 1981.

Pecar, Janez, Gostitve nekaterih deviantnih pojavov v Ljubljani (Spatial distribution of some deviant phenomena in Ljubljana), Institut za kriminologijo, Ljubljana 1975.

Pusic, Evgen, Samoupravljanje (Selfmangement), Narodne novine, Zagreb, 1968.

Pusic Evgen, Opstina i komuna (Municipality and commune), Zagreb, Informator, 1981.

Ribicic, Ciril, (edit), Preoblikovanje krajevnih skuponsti v Ljubljani (Transformation of neighborhood communities in Ljubljana), Ljubljana, 1979.

Seferagic, D., Lay, V., Horvat, B., Lay, I., Caldarovic, O., Drustveni koncept novog neselja (*Social concept of the new settlement*), Institut za drustvena istrazivanja, Sveucilista u Zagrebu, Zagreb, 1981.

Seferagic, Dusica, Suburbane perspektive (*Suburban perspectives*), Revija za sociologiju, Zargeb 1975.

Socioloski aspckti izgradnje gradova (*Sociological aspects of construction of cities*), Savezni zavod za urbanizam i komunalna stambena pitanja, Beograd 1967.

Simovic, vojislav, Komunalni sistem i komunalna politika (*Communal system and communal politics*), NK, Beograd 1966.

SOECO, International Workshop—*Comparative Ecological Analysis of social Change*, FSPN, Ljubljana 1976, I, II, III Vol.

Sarec, Lucka, edit., *Urban Housing Environment*, Urbanisticni institut, Ljubljana 1977.

Sarec, Lucka; Andrej Gulic: Vkljucevanje stanovalcev v urejanje bivalnega okolja v naselju (Participation of inhabitants in shaping of the housing environment), Urbanisticni institut Ljubljana, 1981.

Suvar, Stipe, Izmedju zaseoka i megalopolisa (Between hamlet and megalopolis), Biblioteko "Sociologija sela", Zagreb 1973.

Tomic, Stojarn, The Relationshop between Urbanization and Citizens Participation First International Conference on Participation and Self-Management, Dubrovnik, 1972.

Todorovic, Aleksandar, Uslovi i uzroci mladoletnickog prestupnistva u urbanim i ruralnim sredinama (Conditions and causes of youth delinquency in urban and rural environments), Institut za kriminoloska i socioloska ispitivanja Beograd, 1971.

Urbanizam i sociologija (Urban planning and sociology), Socioloski pregled (special issue), Beograd, 1974/1.

Urbana sociologija (Urban sociology), Revija za sociologijo (special issue), Zagreb 1971.

Vogelnik, Dolfe, Urbanizacija kao odraz privrednog razvoja FNRJ (*Urbanization as a consequence of economic development of Yugoslavia*), Ekonomska biblioteka Beograd, 1961.

Vreg, France, edit: Komuniciranje in odlocanje v delegatskem sistemu (Communications and decision making in delegate-system), DDU Univerzum, Ljubljana 1978.

Vogelnik, Dolfe; Anuska Ferligoj, Slavko Splichal, Urbanization, development and internal migrations in Yugoslavia, *Polish-Yugoslav Seminar*, FSPN, Ljubljana 1980.

Vriser, Igor, Vplivna obmocja jugoslovanskih mest in drugih sredisc (Catchment areas of Yugoslav-towns and other centres), Filozofska fakulteta, Ljubljana 1972.

Vujovic, Sreten; Vladimir Macura et al., Prostorne i socioloske karakteristike i vrednosti novih stambenih naselja u Navom Sadu (Spatial and sociological characteristics and values of the new housing estates in Novi Sad), Jugoslavenski institut za urbanizam i stanovanje, Beograd 1971.

Vujavic, Sreten, Drustvena uslovljenost i drustvene posledice urbanizma

(*Social conditions and consequences of urban planning*), Socioloski pregled, Beograd 1974/1.

Zivkovic, Miroslav et al., Beograd—socioloska studija (Belgrade—sociological research), Institut za kriminoloska i socioloska istrazivanja, Beograd 1977.

Zivkovic, Miroslav, Prilog jugoslovenskoj urbanoj sociologiji (*A contribution to Yugoslav urban sociology*), Zavod za organizaciju poslovanja i obrazovanje kadrova, Beograd 1981.

Zivkovic, Miroslav, Uvod u sociologiju stanovanja (Introduction to sociology of housing), Univerzitet u Beogradu, Beograd 1975.

EIGHTEEN

WOLF HUBER

APPLIED URBAN RESEARCH IN AUSTRIA*

INSTITUTIONAL STRUCTURE OF URBAN RESEARCH IN AUSTRIA

IN AUSTRIA various institutions work in the field of applied urban research:

(1) *municipal departments*, mainly planning departments;

(2) *other public institutions* (federal ministries, state governments, chambers of labour and commerce);

(3) *non-governmental semi-public research institutions*, some of which specially deal with urban and local government problems, such as—

(i) Kommunalwissenschaftliches Dokumentationszentrum (KDZ-Documentation Centre for Urban Studies), Vienna;

(ii) Institut fur Stadtforschung (IS—Institute for Urban Researh), Vienna;

(iii) Institut fur Kommunalwissenschaften (IKW—Institute for Urban Studies), Linz.

Other research institutions working at least to some extent in the field of urban research are—

*Paper presented at the European Meeting on Applied Urban Research, 1981.

(i) Osterreichisches Institut fur Wirtschaftsforschung, Vienna;
(ii) Osterreichisches Institut fur Raumplanung (OIR), Vienna;
(iii) Institut fur Hohere Studien, Vienna;
(iv) Institut fur Umweltforschung, Graz.

(4) *private* researchers and planners, and planning institutions;
(5) *universities* (mainly social science, economics, and planning departments);
(6) research and planning departments of market-oriented *private and public enterprises* (e.g. banks).

Research in planning departments of municipal, state or federal governments or market-oriented enterprises is practically completely done for internal demand. Those urban research programmes worked at by non-governmental research institutions, private researchers or universities are usually *financed* by public institutions. Some of the studies are directly ordered and their results purchased by governmental departments. Most other studies are at least sponsored by grants from governmental departments or public funds.

It is difficult to decide which groups or institutions are the *consumers* or the produced results of urban studies. Only a minor part of the research work is published and thus open for the public. However, one sometimes has the impression that the results are not used by the public institutions, which have ordered or sponsored the studies, either. Of course one cannot expect an immediate impact on political or administrative action. The results need to be discussed in the democratic decision making process. Yet sometimes they do not even seem to stimulate discussion but rather simply fall into oblivion. I think there are some structural factors which can explain these shortcomings.

CRITICAL ASSESSMENT OF APPLIED URBAN RESEARCH—A PERSONAL VIEW

People who have analyzed the practical effectiveness of urban reesearch—and at least "applied" urban research pretends to be practically effective—have usually noticed two facts:

(1) Practitioners and researchers often do not use the same language. Researchers have difficulties to express the results of their studies in a way that helps the politician understand their relevance. Politicians do not make clear what is relevant to them.

(2) There is too much information to be worked up properly. In most cases only a summary of the results can be used for further consideration. And yet there is too little knowledge about things.

In one word: The practical effectiveness of applied urban research is not as high as both practitioners and researchers want it to be. Political practitioners therefore sometimes tend to regard it as useless and are inclined to cut the expenditures for research purposes. Researchers on the other hand sometimes tend to regard practitioners as ignorant.

I believed that the problem has a lot to do with the fact that research is done not only to search for the truth and increase knowledge, but for other purposes as well:

(1) Researchers have been trained in universities and have adopted academic quality standards which are not always the quality standards of practical life. And very often they are aiming at an academic career. Therefore it sometimes seems to be more important to them to publish the results of a study in a scientific journal than to help decision makers solving practical problems.

(2) Politicians on the other hand order studies not merely because they want better information, but also to support their political activities, i.e. for public relation purposes. They do not want the public become informed about

critical results of studies. Besides, financing research is an instrument to make researchers dependent and thus easier to control.

These interest conflicts cane xplain some of the shortcomings of current applied urban research:

(1) A considerable amount of so-called applied research work is not really intended to be applied, but rather to promote the researcher's academic career. It is sponsored simply to keep him busy—and under control.

(2) Many studies the results of which would be practically applicable but do not support the position of the decision makers who pay for it, never reach the public. Therefore it is difficult to assess if and to what extent they have been applied in political or administrative practice.

This assessment of the effectiveness of applied urban research is based on my personal experience in Austria. Yet I would not be surprised to hear that the situation is not much different in other countries.

REFERENCES

Hinzuweisen its auf die Veroffentlichungen des Instituts fur Stadtforschung und des Osterreichischen Instituts fur Raumplanung.

Das Kommunalwissenschaftliche Dokumentationszentrum gibt einen vierteljahrlich erscheinenden Dokumentationsdienst sowie Arbeitshilfen fur die kommunale Praxis heraus, sowie Publikationen zu offentlichen Finanzen, Finanzplanung und Haushaltswesen, Verwaltung und Administration sowie stadtischem Verkehr.

Neuere Veroffentlichungen:

Bauer, H., Brandstetter, E., Goschler, K., *Kommunale Investitionsplane 1979-1982. Ergebnisse der Finanzbedarfserhebung 1979*, Linz 1980 ("Kommunale Forschung in Osterreich," Band 53)

Frohler, L., Kubin E. (eds.), *Privatisierung offentlicher Ausgaben*, Linz 1979 ("Kommunale Forschung in Osterreich", Band 44)

Reorganisation des stadtischen Verkehrs. Mit funfzehn Beitragen von Autoren aus der Bundesrepublik Deutschland, aus Frankreich, den

Niederlanden, aus Schweden, der Schweiz und aus Osterreich. Wien 1981 (KDZ-Arbeitshilfen fur Gemeinden, Nr. 5)

Hier wohnen wir. WohnstraBen: Ein Beitrag zur Wohnumweltverbesserung und Stadterneuerung. Herausgegeben vom Kommunalwissenschaftlichen Dokumentationszentrum im Auftrag des Osterreichischen Nationalkomitees fur die Europaische Kampange fur Stadterneuerung, Wien 1981.

NINETEEN

ARMANDO MONTANARI

METROPOLITAN PLANNING AND PROBLEMS IN EUROPE
The Contribution of the Vienna Centre*

THE VIENNA CENTRE

THE EUROPEAN Coordination Centre for Research and Documentation in Social Sciences (Vienna Centre) is an international non-governmental organisation and an autonomous body of the International Social Science Council.

It was founded in 1963 following a resolution of the XII UNESCO General Conference, and located in Vienna in accordance with an agreement between UNESCO and the Austrian Government.

It aims at facilitating scientific cooperation between social scientists from Eastern and Western Europe in all areas of social sciences.

Its main activities are to coordinate cross-national comparative research projects carried out by participants from Eastern and Western Europe, to organise conferences on topical social science themes, to coordinate a programme of cooperation and exchange of social science information and documentation and to train social scientists in comparative research.

To fulfil its tasks, the Vienna Centre receives financial contributions from Academies of Sciences, Ministries of Education and Science, Social Science Research Councils and

*Paper presented at the European Meeting on Applied Urban Research, 1981.

UNESCO Commissions of 21 European countries. Among them is the Bulgarian Academy of Sciences.

The current research projects of the Vienna Centre are in the following areas:

I. Comparative Analysis, Theory and Evaluation
II. Culture and Family
III. Environment, Urban and Rural Development
IV. Law and Administration
V. Social Policy
VI. Work
VII. Information and Documentation

THE ACTIVITY OF THE VIENNA CENTRE IN THE FIELD OF URBAN DEVELOPMENT

In the area of urban development the Vienna Centre has carried out several projects in the past. The listed publications, even if not directly connected with the subject, has some relevance in the field of urban development also:

Regional Disequilibria in Europe. Backward Areas in Industrial Countries (1968).
Regional Development in Europe (1971)
Foreign Aid to Newly Independent Countries: Problems and Orientations (1971)
Growth Poles and Regional Policies (1972)
The Use of Time: A Cross-national Comparative Survey of Daily Activities of Urban and Suburban Population in Twelve Countries
Juvenile Delinquency. Several publications (1968, 1973, 1975, 1976)
Images of the World in the Year 2000 (1976)
Public policy in temporal perspective. Report on the Workshop on the Application of Time Budget Research to Policy Questions in Urban and Regional Settings (1978)
Urban Europe; A Study of Growth and Decline (1982)

At the moment the Vienna Centre is coordinating two research projects:

(i) the Costs of Urban Growth (CURB)
(ii) The Project Turin International

THE PRESENT ACTIVITY OF THE VIENNA CENTRE IN THE FIELD OF URBAN DEVELOPMENT

The project on the Costs of Urban Growth was set up on 1972, and it is now in the publication stage by Pergamon Press; under the series title of URBAN EUROPE.

The first volume, with the title *A Study of Growth and Decline* was published in February 1982, and deals with the general development of functional urban areas during the period 1950-1975 in the following countries:

Austria, Belgium, Bulgaria, Denmark, France, Federal Republic of Germany, Great Britain, Hungary, Italy, Netherlands, Poland, Sweden, Switzerland, Yugoslavia.

In the first part of the volume a theory of urban development is presented. The theoretical part is followed by Part II in which there are the results of the statistical testing. The third and last part is dedicated to urban policy.

Many other volumes will follow in 1982 and 1983. They will deal with the fundamental and interdependent concepts that currently influence changes in contemporary society. Project Turin was set up on 1980 and now it is only possible to anticipate its research strategy.

Members of the Project Turin are the following cities.

—City of Cologne (Germany, Federal Repupliс of)
—City of Cracow (Poland)
—City of Dresden (German Democratic Republic)
—City of Glasgow (United Kingdom)
—City of Lille (France)

Participants from twenty-nine university and research institutes from 16 European countries have been involved in the CURB project.

Members of the Project Turin are not research or university institutes, as in the CURB case but are 6 East and West European cities. In particular East European cities are mainly using their municipal technical offices for research, also with the help of local and national research institutes. West European cities mainly use the local research and university institutes.

The presence of the cities, with their Lord Mayors. Councillors and City Councils makes a big difference in the way the research is finalised and also in the necessity of prompt utilisation of the results.

For the CURB participants a very important question is what benefit governments can derive from the results of their study. Of course benefits could be that they are forewarned of what the future has in store for them, so that they can take timely measures to mitigate the harmful consequences of autonomous developments.

The members of the Project Turin are directly responsible for their local governments and they have to make a report of their urban policy directly to the City Councils and to their electors.

For this reason the Project Turin will be carried on in a more differentiated way, on the one level a common Project research, and on the other level a series of seminars, conferences and round-tables on different subjects regarding the problems of urban systems.

The first conference of Project Turin with the title *Making the City Work, Enterprise and Democracy in Urban Europe* was organised last October in Glasgow.

The two topics of the Conference were:

(A) Partnership initiative with the private sector
(B) Decentralisation and participation in urban government

To better understand the functioning of the project one has to mention that these two topics were selected for the first conference since the City of Glasgow has launched innovative policies in recent years in both the areas under discussion. The papers and proceedings of the Glasgow Conference will be published in book form.

URBAN GROWTH AND RELATED COSTS

The initiators of the CURB project had to face, from the very beginning, problems connected with the definition of the basic terminology. We do not believe that all the problems connected with urban costs were solved in the CURB project but we consider it useful to mention some of the basic project statements concerning this topic.

Urban Growth may be seen in a triple meaning:

(i) demographic growth, due to population growth
(ii) economical growth, due to the increase of urban products
(iii) spatial growth, due to the territorial expansion

Regarding the differentiations of costs, we should consider:

(i) monetary costs. Housing, transport, sanitation, education etc.
(ii) social costs
(iii) local costs
(iv) non-local costs. Referring to the money used in the areas influenced by the growth.

Considering the quality of costs now, we started from the assumption that it is possible to enumerate four qualitative kinds of costs:

(i) the costs of functioning, necessary to maintain the constant quality of urban services for a number of users, consumers and producers.
(ii) the costs of adaption, corresponding to an extension of the quality of urban services for a constant number of users.
(iii) the costs of growth, needed to maintain the services standard for an increasing number of users.
(iv) the costs of development, corresponding both to an

increasing quality of services and an ever increasing number of users.

It is important to mention this propendent stage of the project also because we have proved with the experience of the CURB project that, while it is relatively easy to identify and describe the costs elements for one or more cities from the same country, it is much more difficult to explain them and extremely difficult to make cross-national comparison. It is only the problem of considering public and private costs, or monetary and social costs, but there is the problem of finding a necessary common point of reference in the different systems of values, of administrative structure, of levels of centralisation or decentralisation, of local governments, of political process and leadership and so on.

For all these difficulties it was then decided to concentrate the attention of the project participants more on investigating factors that shape cities and regions, of characteristics of social, economic and spatial changes and on political implication of processes underlying these changes. Through this the Vienna Centre and the CURB participants contributed to a more meaningful theory of urban growth and also helped the decision-making process more directly. To meet these objectives, the project was structured in two stages.

In stage 1 the research team developed a conceptual framework to incorporate some elements of a behavioural theory of the locational welfare preferences of major decision-agents: households, employers and governments. The evolutionary stages of urban development were then explained in terms of these underlying behavioural postulates. A partial testing of the theory was undertaken at the macro-level of the European urban system for all functional urban regions with a population greater than 200,000 and for all municipalities with a population over 10,000 for a selection of variables over the time period 1950-1975, and the role of multi-faceted urban policies identified and evaluated. This empirical validation at the cross-national scale was further completed by detailed studies of urban change and policy in each participating country, and by a cross-national annotated bibliography of other relevant research.

In stage 2 the research terms developed their activities:

(i) to extend and verify the theoretical framework of urban development and policy and the empirical analysis at the level of individual Functional Urban Regions;

(ii) to measure urban costs over time and space for a wide range of expenditures and to explain them in terms of real indicators of urban growth (population, transport, education,health, recreation, economic services pollution);

(iii) to review how urban systems are financed as a whole and to evaluate current knowledge of costs functions for key stock variables (housing and land, transport and social infrastructure).

For this purpose the following case studies have been analysed:

Amersfoort (NL), Bordeaux (F), Innsbruck (A), Lecco (I), Ljubljana (YU), Lugano (CH), Odense (DK), Olsztyn (PL), Varna (BG), Veszprem (H), Worcester (GB).

THE CITY, CRITICAL DIMENSION

The case of Turin

On the occasion of the seventh Conference of Mayors of Major World Cities which took place in Turin in April 1978, the Centre for Cooperation among World Cities appointed the City Council of Turin to prepare a research plan on the urban problems related to the topic "the city, critical dimension" and to put it at the disposal of other interested cities.

For this purpose a research team was organised in Turin, inviting the more vital forces to collaborate:

(i) the Faculty of Architecture

(ii) the Faculty of Political Sciences

(iii) the Faculty of Economics

(iv) the Faculty of Education, Institute of Sociology.

Industrialists, the Trade Unions and the Cultural Associations were also invited. The Administration of Turin has put the entire city at the disposal of the researchers as a kind of research field or as a big urban laboratory.

The first results of this exercise were put together in a report that was called Project Turin after the name of the City of Turin. Project Turin was structured in seven research studies.

Analysis of the socio-demographic structure of the population
The study put in evidence the presence in Turin of many "parallel cities" that are still waiting for integration to overcome their contradictions and reduce social malaise. With "parallel cities" we mean the different kinds of ghettos present in the City of Turin.

—the city of immigrants, from the South of Italy or from the islands
—the city of dependent workers
—the city of entrepreneurs and professional classes.

From this research it was also found that only 13.5 per cent of the dependent workers were born in Turin whereas 66.3 per cent of the entrepreneurs and professional classes resident in Turin were born in Piedmont.

The frontiers of the city
This research study was focussed on the social services related to urban marginality. The production of social services has been analysed using core studies relative to the following types of urban social marginality:

(i) people discharged from prison
(ii) people discharged from mental hospitals
(iii) the handicapped people
(iv) the drug addicts
(v) the "emarginated" youth

The use of time in an industrialised area
This research study was referred to domestic units, as a kind of measurement unit. This unit was chosen considering the

sociological, economic and anthropological importance the family continues to assume in a country like Italy.

The quality of life and the family behaviour strategies

This research study tried to understand the role of the family in the context of an industrial society and a metropolitan city. How the family changed and how it is now organised. Which are the relationships between the family and the social services and between the family and the city structures.

With this research work it was possible to collect information on the resources of the family and on the selection of expenditure, on the strategy of the family considering, for instance:

(i) the habitation and its use
(ii) the level of social services
(iii) the use of social services and their accessibility
(iv) the political and associative participation, in relationship with the administrative activity carried out at a centralised and decentralised level.

The industry and the higher tertiary sector

Of great relevance for the history of Turin is the history of the origin and the development of its industrial apparatus, dominated by a big car industry (FIAT) to which a system of small and middle sized industries is more or less connected. This research study was chosen because the future of Turin will depend on:

(i) how the industry will transform itself
(ii) how the industry will solve the present element of structural crisis
(iii) how the industry will take its stand in the metropolitan and regional territory.

The future of an industrial city like Turin will also depend on the development of the tertiary sector which, in a developed industrial society, has an evergrowing influence.

The critical size of the city

This wide and difficult subject was considered at the level of decentralised districts. Turin is divided into 23 wards (Consigli di Quartiere), 40-60 thousand inhabitants, and with concrete responsibilities in the management of the territory under their competence.

On the basis it was attempted to make a more correct difinition of the "urban management unit" and its relation to the district systems. A redefinition of the meaning of the term ward and a more precise delineation of its accessibility.

Town planning and urban political instruments

Analysis of the relationship between the town planning, the administrative practice and the local power in Turin and in the period 1945-75. The first indications of this work were already used to take administrative decisions at an operative level. But of course it was considered necessary to separate the research study from the operative level, to allow the researchers to sound out the state of the city without any restrictions. At first it was considered necessary to know the state of the city and to let it be known. It will be subsequently the task of the political forces within the limits of their responsibility, to take the proper decisions to change what was considered distorted in the present situation.

The international project

The experience of the City of Turin was considered a starting point for a research study to be extended to different situations and which should favour a productive cooperation among the city administration which in the meantime joined the project.

In fact no model can be exported, also because no "Model Turin" exists. But an "Experience Cologne, Cracow, Dresden, Glasgow and Lille" exists. Moreover, each of these cities has a common interest in discussing how local governments can contribute to more effective urban policy and in resolving the problems of economic decline.

The city members of the Project Turin are at the moment carrying on a comprehensive research programme based on the following chapters:

Chapter 1: The Economic Structure of Metropolitan Area

Chapter 2: The Impact of Urban Economic Changes on Population Dynamics and Structure

Chapter 3: Analysis of the Labour Market in a Metropolitan Area

Chapter 4: Instruments for the Management of the Spatial Aspects of Change in Urban Economics at the Local Government Level

Chapter 5: Tools of Governing the Local Economy

Chapter 6: Problems of Reorganisation and Reconversion of an Industrial Sector of the Metropolitan Economy

Chapter 7: The Time Budget.

The research studies conducted in Turin until now, and followed by the other member cities of the Project Turin International have convinced the administrators of these large cities that the distorted development of the urban systems are not inevitable.

It is of course a big challange which should result in solidarity of all the city components, administrators and administrated, that operating beyond their inevitable difference have, as a reference point, "the man", with his demands and aspirations.

TWENTY

HACHIRO NAKAMURA

THE BASIS OF URBAN RESEARCH IN JAPAN*

UNTIL about the beginning of 1950's when economic growth of Japan got underway, concern of Japanese people for urban affairs remained rather lukewarm. Since no more concern was shown by academic people, very small portion of them were specialized in urban studies. In some disciplines, say, economics and political science, there were practically none who were interested in urban affairs. Japanese sociology of those days payed a little attention to them, but urban sociologists constituted a minor force whereas rural sociologists occupied a dominant position in terms of their number as well as of the popularity they gained among students.

Return of 1960 population census, however, revealed that the population size of the Densely Inhabited District which is statistically designated as the substantive urban area had outgrown that of other area, urging people to beware the nation of cities was coming of age in Japan. It must be noted here that, as one may learn from U.N. Demographic Yearbook, Japan gives a rather strict definition of the city compared to many other countries. Conditions are even more strictly difined for an area to be included in DID.

In themean while many sorts of urban problems were sprouting and grew more and more serious, while urban discontent

*Paper presented at the European Meeting on Applied Urban Research, 1981.

and severe criticism on the governmental policy for urban affairs were spreading among urban people. Since Japanese people were thus faced with a new challenge, ever increasing number of them, whether they are in governmental sector, political circles, business firms, academic world, the press and so on, are paying their sincere attention to urban problems. Multifarious devices and attempts have been made to cope with these emerging problems and urban studies are now in a state of booming accordingly.

It is rather difficult to give an account of the situation in detail regarding urban studies in Japan because they keep on mushrooming today, but the introduction given hereafter may serve, I hope, as a clue to guess what is going on in Japan so far as urban studies are concerned.

INSTITUTIONS

Governmental sector

The Ministry of Construction;
The Ministry of Home Affairs;
National Land Agency;
Environmental Agency;
The Ministry of Health and Welfare;
Economic Planning Agency;

These above are concerned with urban affairs in matters of which they are respectively in charge. ANL and EA were established when land problems and environmental problems grew serious with the rapid progress of urbanization.

All of these governmental organizations very often conduct censuses and surveys and publish their findings. In addition, there are many local governments that conduct surveys and opinion researches providing data to be used for urban studies.

Research institute

(a) National institute or institute established as a special corporation financed by the national budget (shown in each parenthesis is the name of ministry or agency the institute is attached to)

Population Problems Research Institute (Ministry of Health and Welfare)

Social Development Research Institute (Ministry of Health and Welfare)

Local Government Research and Data Center (Ministry of Home Affairs)

National Consumer Information Center (Economic Planning Agency)

These Institutes advance studies that are regarded as bases for the policy of the ministries and agencies to which they are attached to.

(b) Research institutes established as foundations.

The Tokyo Institute for Municipal Research
The Japan Center for Area Development
There are a number of other institutes of this categories. Of these two well-know institutes, the former was established more than fifty years ago, and has a long tradition of urban research in Japan.

(c) Research institutes called "Think Tank"

Out of the growing concern for urban affairs, increasing number of the research institute of this type have been established recently in Japan. Mostly they conduct research as their business, that is, to perform a contract received from governmental organizations and business firms. Sphere of their researches are not confined to urban affairs, but urban studies consitute one of the main fields of their activities. A few of the most well-known are as follows:

National Institute for Research Advancement (NIRA)
Nomura Research Institute
Mitsubishi Research Institute, Inc.

Universities

So far as Universities are concerned, Researches are mostly carried out by individual professors or by a group of professors spontaneously organized. If a proposed research project is deemed qualified, funds are available through the Ministry of Education or number of foundations of which the Toyoda Foundation is outstanding. An appropriate professor is often asked by governmental organizations or research institute of any type to take part in their research projects.

A number of universities, national, municipal or private, have established research institutes as their annex, many of which pursue studies related with urban problems in one way or another. A few of them are specialized in the urban study as is the case with the Urban Study Center of the Tokyo Metropolitan University and the Capital Region Research Institute of the International Christan University.

CENSUS AND SURVEY DATA

As for the statistical data available for and of use to the urban studies in Japan, main ones are as follows:

- Population Census
- Housing Census
- Census of Commerce
- Census of Factories
- Establishment Census
- Monthly Labour Statistics
- Population Movement Statistics
- Consumer Statistics

While these are data turned out by the national government, local governments also provide data as the findings of surveys they have conducted. Large-scale opinion surveys are very often carried out by government or semi-governmental bodies. Public Opinion Research Section of the Prime Minister's Office collects the findings of these surveys and publishes Yearbook of Public Opinion Survey to show the outline of them. Although a volume of other data is available, the number of them is so great and the kinds of them are so many that I cannot afford to refer to them in this brief introduction.

PART PLAYED BY URBAN STUDY

One may classify the purposes of urban research in Japan into three categories; (1) for policy formation, (2) for business enterprise, and (3) for scientific or theoretical exploration. Generally speaking, the 1st type is aimed at by the governmental sector, the 2nd by the research institutes of the Think Tank type and the 3rd by other institutes and universities. But just as the distinction between research and survey is practically not so clear cut as is made in a text-book on the social research. The above classification does not always remain rigid. Whereas the return of census and survey for policy formation provides basic data available for the scientific study as well as for business opportunities, current policies of governmental sector and political strategies of a particular political party very often influence the research projects and the analytical viewpoint of those who are supposed to pursue the scientific study, and this, in turn, reacts-upon governmental sectors and political parties more often than not. In the worst case, this caused an existing popular bias even more distorted in Japan where detached way of observation and analysis is rather poorly developed among social scientists.

On the other hand, it so happened that a certain topic of academic urban study attracted the attention of governmental sectors and influenced their policy. What falls on this case is the community. It used to be discussed on only in the academic circle, but today a grave importance is given to it in the policy of governmental sector. In particular the Ministry of Home Affairs which interprets the community in a normative meaning provided measures to create it. Many local governments are endeavoring to comply with this policy.

INDEX

Agregate comparative statistics, 97
Agricultural processing industry, 115
Alford, Robert, 73
Amsterdam, 108, 182; urban agglomeration, 182
Appalachian Piedmont, 41
Australia, 114; pacific, 41
Austria, applied urban research, 191-96
Autobahan system, 95

Back to the city, movement, of 130-31
Balkanization, 4
Belgium, 72
Beograd, 187
Bemi, Hamm, 8
Berge, Erling, 10, 59
Berlin, German Urban Institute, 162
Berry, B.J.L., 1, 55, 60
Blocking urban renewal programmes, 110
Blue-collar workers, 122
Bodenschatz, Harald, 107
Bolting, Horest M., 15, 149
Brease, G., 2
Britain, Standard Industrial Classification (SIC), 89; Inner cities research programme, 143; inner metropolitan migration, 144
British inner cities research programme, 145; regional policy, 97
Budapest, 56

Cantons, fiscal system, 174
Capitalist and socialistic countries, urban development in, 56
Central Business Districts (CBD), 129
Clark, Gardner, 173
Clark, J.N., 2
Comparative Research, problems of, 53-55; process, 73
Comparative urban analysis, 23; methods of 23; classification of, 25; purpose of, 24-26; fragmentation of, 3; importance of, 6; progress in, 53; proliferation of, 3
Conceptual equivalence, 6
Conducting research, agencies for, 169
Continuing population deconcentration, 127
Cordon sanitaire, 45
Critical dimension, 203
Cross national comparative research, 11, 18, 61
Cultural genetic approaches, 39-40, 44; development of, 9; variations, 38
Current research priorities, 14; trends, 137
CURB participants, 200; project, 199
CUS, purpose of, 29

Daland, R.T., 1, 5
Decision-oriented research, 149
Derelict land, 89

Densely Inhabited District (DID), 209
Dominion capitalist societies, 114
Duncan, O.D., 34

Economic competition dictate policies, 131
Ellesmere Pert, 95
England, urban renewal in, 109
Environmental damage, 138; factors, 74
Europe, higher tertiary sector, 205; international project, 206; metropolitan planning and problems, 197; urban systems, 202; industrialised area, 204
Evaluation research, findings of, 150; problems, 15
Exurban, 129

Federal Ministry for Regional Planning, Building and Urban Development, 151, 153
Federal Reform Programmes, 159
Federal Republic of Germany, 85, 149; practice-oriented evaluation research, 152; problems, 150; regional planning and urban development, 153
Foreign Policies, environment of, 79
France, 145; educational system, 140; research programmes in, 167-70, 145; private sector, 145
Friderichs, Jurgen, 9, 53
Functional urban regions, 199, 203

German federal system, 159; political science association, 157-163
Germani, G., 1
Germany, 72; applied urban research in, 157-63; urban research programme, 163
Gibbs, J.P., 34
Giddens, A., 113
Ginic, I., 185

Glasgow Conference, 200
Greenbelts, 128

Hahn, F.G., 39
Hamburg, 56
Hamm, B., 23, 31
Hawley, Ames H., 60
Heise, Volker, 107
Hofmeister, B., 37, 40
Holland, migration process, 144
Holzner, L., 38, 42
Home-centered communities, 130
Homogeneity-heterogeneity problem, 29
Huber, Wolf, 191
Hunter, A., 33
Huttenlocher, 39

Improve future comparatives research, 10
Internal spatial distribution, 64
International comparative research, problems of, 86, 87; social science research, 89; methodological problems of, 107
International conferences, 70; languages, 69

Japan, Densely inhabited district, 209; environmental problems, 210; governmental sector, 210; Research institutes, 210

Kasarda, John D., 14, 60, 119
Kerl-Heinz Simon, 8
Konrad, G., 113
Kunzmann, Klaus R., 12
Latif, A.H., 33
Large cities, functional transformations of, 128

Latin-American culture region, 41, 42
Leichter, Howard M., 67, 79
Lichtenberger, E., 44

Ljubljana, (urban research universities), 187
London, 56, 108

MacRae, Duncan Jr., 75
Macura, V., 187
McDermott, P., 116
McGee, T.G., 44
Medows, P., 1
Mellor, R.E.H., 44
Merseyside, 90, 91-93, 97, 100; structure of, 94
Methodological approach, 11; issues, 97; problems, 23
Metropolitan and urban level, 95, 142
Micro-climate, 128
Mlinar, Z., 185
Monodisciplinary approach, 76
Montainari, Armando, 18, 197
Muller, P.O., 127
Multi-level systems, problems of, 62
Mutual-scale economies, 123

Nakamura, Hichiro, 18, 209
National Research Programme, 140
National urban policies, 129, 132; system, 69, 140
Natural sciences, 38
Neighbouring disciplines, 185
Netherlands, 143; inner cities research programme, 143; National Physical Planning Agency, 181; urban research in, 181; some major issues, 181
New urban policies, 130; realities, 119-128
New York white-collar professional, 126
New Zealand, 114, 115; rationalise agricultural processing, 115
Noguchi, T., 127
Noise buffers, 128
Non-actor systems, 16, 62
Non-metropolitan blue-collar, 129
North America, metropolitan core cities in, 119
Norton, Alan, 67

Oberhummer, E., 40
Odum, H., 128
Old Industrial Agglomerations, 88-105; regions, 93

Paris, 56
Parochialism, 3
Passarge, S., 40
Pedestrian-safe complexes, 129
Pilot project, 86, 92
Poland, 72
Policy analysis, 73-77; comparative studies in, 77-79; modification of, 13; comparison, rationale for, 81-82; discription, 80; problems, 11
Political decision-making processes, 92
Polycentric agglomeration, 91
Popper, Karl R., 74
Population pressure, 77; socio-demographic structure of, 204
Project Turin, 199-200
Przeworski, A., 6
Public policies, 79, 142, 145

Queensland, population movements, 116
Quinn, A., 33

Regional development, alternative strategies of, 139; and inter-regional level, 139; problems, research in, 138-42; planning, 16
Ribicic, C., 186
Robert, Jacques, 137
Roterdam, 108; urban agglomeration, 182
Ruhrgebiet, 90, 91, 93, 95, 97, 100; structures of, 94
RUHR-MERSEY-Project, 86

Sarajevo, 187
Schneider, J., 127
Second World War, 173
Segregated economic waste lands, 130
Slum landlordism, 110
Socio-ecological explanations, 59-64; economic class structure, 77; spatial differentiation, 32
Special emphasis programme, 17
Stewart, J.D., 78
Stillwell, F.J., 116
Structural economic change, process of, 12-16, 85-90; unemployment, 131
Suburban, 129; development, 97; shopping centre, 123
Suburbanization, 183
Suvar, S., 185
Sweden, 144; inner-metropolitan migration, 144; long-term planning, 146
Swiss national Science Foundation, 17; urban research, 177; urban system, 173
Switzerland, 16, 144; inner-metropolitan migration, 144; large comparative urban research, 175-76; urban community research in, 173-78
Szelenyi, I., 113

Tilly, C., 2
Transnational and comparative research constraints of, 146-47
Transport infrastructure, 96
Transportation technologies, 121-23
Tremendous problems, 56
Theoretical and methodological issues, 99-105
Throns, David C., 13, 113

Ultramodern industrial parks, 124
Underlying employment problems, ameliorate symptoms of, 132
UNESCO, 197-98
Unique problems, 68
United Nations, development programme, 70; decentralized locations, advantage of, 122; middle income population, 119; national urban policy, 126; telecommunication revolution, 123; transportation distribution technologies, 122; urban policies, failure of, 120
Urban agglomeration, 174, 176, 181; development, comparative analysis of, 13; differentiation, dimensions of, 30-33; and metropolitan development strategies, research in, 143; and metropolitan problems, 142
Urban policies, 131; primarily focussing on, 186; instruments, 206; problems, internationalisation of, 113; sorts of, 209; special emphasis programme on, 178; varieties of, 7; renaissance, 124-28
Urban renewal, programmes, 56-58; organisation of, 107-8; revitalization and renovation, 181
Urban research, 14-18, 159, 160; agenda of, 161; conference, 160-62; focussing, 158; national political climate for, 177
Urban structure, 100-105: cross-cultural studies of, 44-46; current problems, 57; description of, 33; methodological problems of, 100-103
Urban social movements, 109; Sociology, 185
Urban-targeted welfare programme, 129
Urbanization-migration process, 1, 173, 186; universal process of, 46

Value systems, 73
Verba, Siolney, 74
Vickers, Geoffrey, 79
Vienna centre, 56, 197-98; present activity of, 199; urban development, field of, 193-202
Vogelnik, D., 185
Volkswagen Foundation, 163
Voogid, Hemk, 181
Vujovic, S., 187

Wallestein, Immanuel, 62
Walton, J., 1, 2, 4
Wasocti, L.H., 4
Waste absorption, 128
Water quality control, 128
West Berlin, 108
West Germany 109, 141; urban and regional planning, 141; long-term urban planning, 146
White-collar-Job, 124
Wollmann, Hellmut, 16, 157
World Health Organisation, 70

Yadav, C.S., 1
Yugoslav Sociological Association, 187
Yugoslavia, 17; urban social research in, 185; decentralization process of, 186
Youth unemployment, 94
Zagreb, 187

Zimmerman, Erwin, 16, 173
Zivkovic, M., 186